LEADERSHIP AND MANAGEMENT CHALLENGES OF IN-HOUSE LEGAL COUNSEL

Edited by
Benny S. Tabalujan

BEc, LLB (Monash), LLM, PhD (Melbourne), MSID

Barrister and Solicitor, Supreme Court of Victoria and High Court of Australia

Adjunct Faculty (Associate Professor), Melbourne Business School and Melbourne Law School, The University of Melbourne

LexisNexis Butterworths
Australia
2008

LexisNexis

AUSTRALIA	LexisNexis Butterworths 475–495 Victoria Avenue, CHATSWOOD NSW 2067 On the internet at: www.lexisnexis.com.au
ARGENTINA	LexisNexis Argentina, BUENOS AIRES
AUSTRIA	LexisNexis Verlag ARD Orac GmbH & Co KG, VIENNA
BRAZIL	LexisNexis Latin America, SAO PAULO
CANADA	LexisNexis Canada, Markham, ONTARIO
CHILE	LexisNexis Chile, SANTIAGO
CHINA	LexisNexis China, BEIJING, SHANGHAI
CZECH REPUBLIC	Nakladatelství Orac sro, PRAGUE
FRANCE	LexisNexis SA, PARIS
GERMANY	LexisNexis Germany, FRANKFURT
HONG KONG	LexisNexis Hong Kong, HONG KONG
HUNGARY	HVG-Orac, BUDAPEST
INDIA	LexisNexis, NEW DELHI
ITALY	Dott A Giuffrè Editore SpA, MILAN
JAPAN	LexisNexis Japan KK, TOKYO
KOREA	LexisNexis, SEOUL
MALAYSIA	Malayan Law Journal Sdn Bhd, SELANGOR DURAL EHSAN
NEW ZEALAND	LexisNexis, WELLINGTON
POLAND	Wydawnictwo Prawnicze LexisNexis, WARSAW
SINGAPORE	LexisNexis, SINGAPORE
SOUTH AFRICA	LexisNexis Butterworths, DURBAN
SWITZERLAND	Staempfli Verlag AG, BERNE
TAIWAN	LexisNexis, TAIWAN
UNITED KINGDOM	LexisNexis UK, LONDON, EDINBURGH
USA	LexisNexis Group, New York, NEW YORK LexisNexis, Miamisburg, OHIO

National Library of Australia Cataloguing-in-Publication entry

Author:	Tabalujan, Benny S.
Title:	Leadership and management challenges of in-house legal counsel.
Edition:	1st edition.
ISBN:	9780409325249 (pbk).
Notes:	Includes index.
Subjects:	Corporate legal departments. Attorney and client. Legal ethics.
Dewey Number:	346.066.

© 2008 Reed International Books Australia Pty Limited trading as LexisNexis

Typeset in Bembo, Gill Sans and Optima.

Typeset by Palmer Higgs. Printed in Australia by Ligare Pty Ltd (NSW).

Visit LexisNexis Butterworths at www.lexisnexis.com.au

FOREWORD

I have had the privilege of serving as patron of the New South
Wales division of ACLA for more than 20 years. Together with my
service as a judge of the Supreme Court of New South Wales in
charge of the commercial work of the court and subsequently as a
director on a number of boards and as a consultant to a major
Australian law firm, I have had a box seat in watching with keen
interest the evolution of in-house counsel.

In all honesty, I have to admit that there was a time many years ago
when the position of in-house counsel was filled with people who
should (rather charitably) be described as not in the front rank of
legal practitioners. It is a great pleasure for me to say that we have
gone from one extreme to the other. Some of the foremost lawyers in
Australia have lent their skills to organisations as in-house counsel.
Many have gone on to use their knowledge and experience to join
the senior executive ranks of large corporations.

There is now a flourishing industry in seminars and conferences at
which luminaries offer insights as to the best methods for in-house
counsel to discharge their duties. Similarly, much attention is paid as
to how external counsel should deal with (not to mention solicit
work from) their in-house counterparts. However, as far as I am
aware, *Leadership & Management Challenges of In-house Legal Counsel*,
edited by Dr Benny Tabalujan, is the first book in Australia where
highly qualified and eminent in-house counsel and consultants have
specifically focused on the in-house legal role.

The very title of the book and the quality of the individual
chapter contributions indicate the breadth of questions which
confront in-house counsel today. In particular, it is pleasing to see a
contribution from a senior government lawyer highlighting the
contrasts and similarities of the role of in-house counsel in

government service. In another chapter, when one looks at the question of in-house counsel as in-house conscience, it is challenging to consider the kinds of ethical problems confronting in-house counsel in a profit-making organisation.

It is also interesting to note that — notwithstanding obvious cultural differences — many of the challenges of in-house counsel are replicated in other jurisdictions. This is brought out in the chapter by Mr Chua Lee Ming, based on his experience as General Counsel to the Government of Singapore Investment Corporation. The point is made even more explicit by Ms Edith Shih from Hong Kong, who leads a global team of around 200 in-house counsel within the Hutchison Whampoa group of companies.

At the bottom of all this lies the perennial problem. On the one hand, the enjoinder to in-house counsel is to know the business inside out, to use their legal expertise to advance corporate goals. On the other hand, they are also called to maintain their objectivity and, above all, their independence. This last requirement is still subject to continuous judicial examination in the context of claims of privilege.

Like this perennial problem, none of the topics subjected to examination in this book will have final answers. The role of in-house counsel continues to evolve. It is the subject of scrutiny not least by in-house counsel themselves. Dare I say they will be considerably assisted and challenged in this task by the contributions in this book.

As someone once remarked: a lecture is worthwhile if one leaves afterwards better informed. I am sure the readers of this book will have that rewarding experience.

The Honourable Andrew Rogers, QC
Sydney, August 2008

CONTENTS

Foreword   v
Preface   ix
Glossary of Terms   xiii

PART 1   The Context

1 **Setting the Scene: Challenges for the In-house
   Counsel Role**   3
   Peter Turner, CEO, Australian Corporate Lawyers Association

PART 2   Managing Self

2 **Transitioning from External Counsel to In-house
   Counsel**   23
   Chua Lee Ming, General Counsel, Government of Singapore Investment
   Corporation Pte Ltd; Vice President, Singapore Corporate Counsel Association

3 **Managing In-house Counsel Workload**   34
   Benny Tabalujan, Associate Professor, Melbourne Business School;
   Director, IKD

4 **Professional Development for In-house Counsel:
   What's Next?**   47
   Jil Toovey, Director, IKD

PART 3   Leading the Legal Team

5 **Strategic Leadership for the In-house Legal Team**   65
   Will Irving, Group General Counsel, Telstra Corporation Ltd

6 **The Government In-house Legal Role: Similarities,
   Contrasts and Challenges**   85
   Bruce Brown, Special Counsel, Commonwealth of Australia Department
   of Finance and Deregulation

7 One Day of Leading a Global Legal Team   **100**
Edith Shih, Head Group General Counsel and Company Secretary,
Hutchison Whampoa Ltd

**8 Evaluating the Performance of In-house
Legal Teams**   **114**
Benny Tabalujan, Associate Professor, Melbourne Business School;
Director, IKD

Christopher Lloyd, Professor of Business Statistics,
Melbourne Business School

**PART 4   Responding to Internal and External
Environments**

9 Commerciality: Partnering with Internal Clients   **129**
Debby King-Rowley, Principal, Burlington Consulting
Kirsten Dale, Consultant, IKD

**10 Professional Ethics: In-house Counsel as In-house
Conscience**   **141**
Kirsten Mander, General Counsel and Company Secretary,
Sigma Pharmaceuticals Ltd

11 What In-house Counsel want from Law Firms   **157**
Ronald F Pol, Director, Team Factors Ltd

Index   175

PREFACE

The seeds of this book started to germinate in 2006. By that time, I had been undertaking consulting work for several years with Melbourne-based IKD — then still a wholly-owned subsidiary of Australian law firm Freehills. Through that work, I had come into contact with many in-house legal counsel. It was then that I began to notice the relative dearth of books on the in-house legal role.

In early 2007, I floated the idea for this book with Will Irving, Group General Counsel at Telstra. He was wholly supportive. Within a short time, commitments were received from other interested contributors. LexisNexis Butterworths was sufficiently intrigued to offer a publishing contract. Over subsequent months, what had started out as a project for a small volume focusing on Australian in-house counsel broadened to include contributions providing Asia-Pacific perspectives from New Zealand, Singapore and Hong Kong.

In compiling this book, I have intentionally focused on the leadership and management challenges faced by in-house counsel. All of the contributors have also adopted this approach, generally steering clear of black-letter law issues. The reason for this is simple. Many of the in-house legal counsel I have met felt that these 'softer' aspects of their role have not been researched or discussed in-depth. Yet, as in-house legal teams grow in importance and size within their respective organisations, these softer aspects have become very significant issues. So it is this gap that this book is intended to help fill.

The existence of this gap itself is somewhat puzzling. Around a quarter of Australia's practising lawyers are working in-house; yet there was (and still is) relatively little published material on the challenges they face. Indeed, to my knowledge, this is the first book published in Australia which is wholly dedicated to the in-house legal profession.

Today, Australian in-house legal teams range in size from small to large. The largest teams comprise more than 100 lawyers (as in the case of the legal team at Telstra). Size aside, Australian in-house counsel are increasingly playing more significant roles in their organisations — even more so as financial markets and the global economy become more volatile. Many have become trusted advisers and leaders in their own right. Among the larger legal teams, some control legal budgets of tens of millions of dollars. In every case, the perennial challenge is still how to manage and undertake the legal function so as to maximise its impact and contribution to the organisation.

In structure, this book is broadly divided into four parts. In Part 1, Peter Turner, Chief Executive of ACLA, sets the scene by sketching the current environment facing in-house legal counsel. Peter does an admirable job in giving an overview of how the in-house legal profession has developed, the present challenges facing it, and the likely trends for the future.

In Part 2, we delve into the micro level by focusing on the in-house legal counsel as an individual professional. Chua Lee Ming, General Counsel to the Government of Singapore Investment Corporation, offers insights as to the mindset and behavioural changes which lawyers from private practice are often required to make when they move in-house. Once ensconced in-house, there is the constant challenge of managing an enormous and varied workload — this is the subject of a separate chapter which I write drawing on my work with in-house legal teams. Then Jil Toovey from IKD focuses on what professional development programs in-house counsel require if they are to progress further in their careers.

In Part 3 of the book, the chapters share a common theme of how best to lead a legal team. Will Irving contributes a lucid chapter on strategic leadership issues faced by the in-house function. Bruce Brown, Special Counsel for the Australian Department of Finance and Deregulation, highlights the similarities and differences of working in-house for a business corporation compared to being a government lawyer. Then Edith Shih, from Hutchison Whampoa in Hong Kong, offers a rare insight as to what one day looks like in the life of a general counsel leading a global legal team. I wrote the last chapter in this section with my Melbourne Business School colleague, Chris Lloyd, as we examine the challenge of measuring the performance of in-house legal teams.

In Part 4 of the book, the contributors focus on how in-house legal counsel are responding to changes in the internal and external environments in which they operate. Debby King-Rowley and Kirsten Dale, who undertook research into 'commerciality intelligence' among lawyers, provide an overview of their research findings. Kirsten Mander then discusses the role of in-house legal counsel as the in-house conscience — how this role can be full of tension and ethical dilemmas. Finally, Ronald Pol, a past President of CLANZ, writes an insightful chapter on what in-house legal counsel really want from law firms.

Clearly, a book like this — which brings together the talents and experiences of such a broad range of contributors from Australia and the Asia-Pacific region — owes much to many people. For that reason, I am delighted to acknowledge publicly the contribution of each chapter contributor. Each one has been a pleasure to work with. Each took time from a very busy schedule to pen words which hopefully will benefit our readers. For that alone, I am grateful to each of them.

It should be noted that each contributor has been particularly helpful in providing the sources cited in their chapters. Some have gone to great lengths to provide these references. While every care has been taken to establish and acknowledge the copyright of others, the publishers and chapter contributors will be happy to correct any inadvertent oversight on this point.

I am also grateful to Joanne Beckett at LexisNexis Butterworths for guiding this book to publication. Her quick mind spotted the potential for the book from the very beginning, and her calmness throughout the writing and editorial stages was reassuring. I wish to also thank The Honourable Andrew Rogers QC, patron of the New South Wales division of ACLA, who kindly wrote the Foreword. Thanks also should go to Georgia O'Neill who undertook the final editorial work on behalf of LexisNexis — in what must be a near record timeframe.

It would be remiss of me not to also thank Janet Russell, former Managing Director of IKD, and Jil Toovey, Director of IKD, as well as all my IKD colleagues — past and present — for their indirect help in bringing this book to fruition. It was through IKD that I began to develop a deep interest in the in-house legal role, one that still continues today. I must also thank all the in-house counsel I have come across through my work with IKD; many have contributed valuable ideas and insights — some of which are now reflected in this book.

Finally, and by no means least, I must thank my wife Pauline who still continues to support and encourage me as I take on yet another writing project; she is a gem.

My hope for this book is that it will be of some benefit to every in-house legal counsel who takes time to read it. If it provides just one insight which makes the working life of in-house counsel more pleasant, more productive or more meaningful, or if it spurs additional research into the in-house legal role, then the effort of compiling, editing and producing this volume has been worthwhile.

This book is dedicated to all in-house legal counsel who strive to make a positive difference in their organisations.

Benny S Tabalujan
Melbourne Business School
September 2008

He has showed you, O man, what is good.
And what does the Lord require of you?
To act justly and to love mercy and to walk humbly with your God.
(Micah 6:8 NIV)

GLOSSARY OF TERMS

ACC: Association of Corporate Counsel

ACCC: Australian Competition and Consumer Commission

ACLA: Australian Corporate Lawyers Association

AGM: Annual General Meeting

AICD: Australian Institute of Company Directors

AIM: Alternative Investment Market

ALRC: Australian Law Reform Commission

ASIC: Australian Securities and Investments Commission

CLANZ: Corporate Lawyers Association of New Zealand

CEO: Chief Executive Officer

CFO: Chief Financial Officer

CLE: Continuing Legal Education

COO: Chief Operating Officer

CSA: Chartered Secretaries Australia

CTO: Chief Technology Officer

FCIS: Fellow, Chartered Institute of Secretaries

FTE: Fulltime equivalent

HR: Human resource

KPI: Key performance indicator

KRA: Key result area

ROI: Return on investment

INSTITUTE OF KNOWLEDGE DEVELOPMENT

IKD was established in 1999 as a subsidiary of Freehills. Today, IKD is an independent niche consultancy providing innovative learning & development programs and consulting services to a range of professionals, with a focus on lawyers and in-house legal counsel.

LCEDP – Legal Counsel Executive Development Program
LMP – Lawyers Management Program
LEAP – Lawyers as Educators and Presenters
CQ – Building Commerciality Intelligence
Executive Coaching
Legal team off-sites and conferences
The Road to General Counsel
LegalScores – the in-house legal team performance index

IKD Pty Ltd
PO Box 18086 Collins St Melbourne Vic 8003 Australia
T 61 1300 668 353 F 61 3 9806 1205

www.ikd.com.au

PART 1

The Context

1

SETTING THE SCENE: CHALLENGES FOR THE IN-HOUSE COUNSEL ROLE

by

Peter Turner[*]

Peter Turner is the CEO of ACLA — the professional association for both private and public sector in-house counsel in Australia. He was previously Vice President, Legal Affairs at Foster's Group Ltd and before that worked overseas as senior in-house counsel for Royal Philips Electronics Group. He is a former chair of the Corporate Counsel Forum of the International Bar Association and is currently on its Advisory Board. He holds Law and Arts degrees from the University of Melbourne and an MBA from Sophia University, Tokyo.

Introduction

As in many other jurisdictions, the last few decades have seen unprecedented growth in the number and proportion of lawyers in the Australian legal profession who practise in-house in both the public and private sectors. Of the estimated 50,000 lawyers currently in practice throughout Australia, around a quarter are employed in-house.

According to a survey conducted recently for the Law Society of New South Wales, the percentage of lawyers currently practising in-house in that state is almost 27%.[1] Another survey estimates that by 2015 that percentage will have risen to over 30%.[2] There is every reason to think that these figures will eventually translate nationally.

Importantly, this expected growth in numbers seems underpinned by a strong, if not booming, jobs market for those who wish to practise in-house. Not only are positions now vacant across the entire range of in-house practice, but the salaries and conditions offered for in-house roles have moved up to an extent that in-house positions — particularly in the private sector — now attract the very best candidates from all points of the legal compass.

According to the most recent Mahlab Corporate Survey:[3]

> [T]he corporate sector remains a very attractive option for lawyers. 52% of private practice lawyers surveyed advised that they were considering moving from their current role. 1 in 5 respondents indicated that they viewed an in-house role as the next step in their career. An in-house role offers a high degree of satisfaction with almost 80% of those surveyed stating they were very or somewhat satisfied in their current role.

But so much for the good news! This chapter addresses some key challenges to the in-house role. Its basic tenet is that the strong growth of the in-house legal sector in recent years may be difficult to maintain as we move further into the twenty-first century. This bad news can perhaps best be encapsulated in the old adage that 'what goes up must come down'. The reality is that any way you look at it there is a whole range of challenges looming for in-house practice. While no single unmet challenge would immediately diminish in-house practice as we know it, a combination of them could be very damaging indeed.

To predict the future, it is always helpful to examine the past and see what we can learn from it. The early part of this chapter therefore does that and then looks at what the future might hold. The chapter goes on to identify some significant challenges specific to in-house practice and then looks at certain issues facing business (including the business of government) and seeks to predict how they might influence the future of in-house practice. Last but not least, the chapter identifies some professional challenges which could severely impact on the future of in-house practice in Australia.

Learning from the past

The history of in-house legal practice in Australia and overseas has taught us conclusively that the client is king and that kings always require value for money. Establishing their value has therefore been a threshold issue for in-house counsel everywhere.

In the early years of in-house practice in Australia, during the 1950s and 1960s, the focus of the corporate legal profession was still primarily on solving legal problems on a case-by-case, curative basis. Important matters were referred for an opinion to external lawyers or to bar counsel as they arose. The few practitioners who practised in-house were regarded askance by both business and the profession and were often treated as legally-trained clerks to whom only routine legal tasks could be referred. Real problems required 'real' lawyers — that is, from the profession.

On the other hand, neither the profession nor indeed many of the first 'in-housers' knew much about their clients' business or their business strategies. They saw few of the many opportunities that were inherent in the business process for managing risk and adding value. In government departments and agencies, ministers relied almost exclusively on legal advice from the protected monopolies of the Crown Solicitor's Offices.

However, as the economic importance of Australia's financial, mining and industrial sectors grew and as the country increasingly opened up for foreign investment and began expanding overseas, deal making and investment opportunities grew in frequency and significance. The globalisation of business and consequent hyper-competition led to heightened levels of business activity, including a move towards corporatisation within government.

During the 1980s and 1990s the corporate and legal landscape changed quite distinctively as long-established Australian businesses fell into new (often overseas) hands, and entrepreneurs played havoc with a lax regulatory regime. As we all know, however, following a spate of spectacular corporate collapses in the early 1990s, many new laws and regulations were passed which re-regulated the corporate sector and better protected consumers. 'Compliance' and 'governance' became the buzz words of that new era — a mantra that stifled some corporate adventures but fed a hungry legal profession.

It was in this more complex legal and economically active commercial environment that the role of the in-house practitioner, as we now know it in Australia, began to assume its current form. Experiments had been carried out by some organisations in in-sourcing large chunks of their legal work. Others had tried hiring a senior legal officer to manage their legal issues. Some traditional government legal monopolies had been opened up to external competition or to supervision by newly appointed in-house government lawyers hired directly by the agency, department or minister concerned.

Of course, not all these experiments proved successful. The trend to in-sourcing was neither popular nor appreciated in all quarters. As a consequence, there were some dramatic cases of entire legal departments suddenly again being outsourced. Some newly established in-house departments simply folded due to unexpected structural problems or sheer inexperience.

Slowly but surely, however, in-house practice and in-house legal departments began making a real impact. Business people and bureaucrats began to see that having on tap in-house legal counsel — individuals who really understood and were committed to the business and the mission of the organisation — had significant advantages. In short, savvy in-house counsel brought real business understanding, tailored advice on legal risk and compliance, and legal engineering to harried executives at dramatically reduced cost. Gradually, in-house counsel became essential members of corporate and government executive teams, the 'right hands' of CEOs and, eventually, 'the keepers of the corporate conscience' in organisations right across Australia.

The primary lesson from this colourful past is that while legal practice in-house in Australia has now definitely come of age, to remain competitive in future the in-house profession will need to constantly adapt and change as increasingly complex legal and business landscapes continue to unfold. For one thing, over the years, the cost differential between external and in-house lawyers has narrowed. It is likely to narrow still further in the future.

While the commercial emphasis is already very much more on value than cost, adding demonstrable value to businesses operating in a climate of constant change has, unfortunately, become increasingly difficult. The introduction of new, dedicated in-house legal technology was once thought likely to provide some particular opportunities in that regard, but it is now clear that that path offers no panacea. The fact is that without the involvement of real lawyers, technological solutions — particularly over time — tend to homogenise outcomes rather than to add value.

It is now also clear that some greenfield areas of in-house practice, such as those concerned with corporate social and corporate governance responsibilities, are not the exclusive province of in-house lawyers. Today, there is a veritable army of external lawyers and consultants who are keen to take over those responsibilities. Risk and crisis management, compliance and intellectual property are other areas of in-house legal practice that are or could be in the same boat. On the other hand, brand management, financial regulation and many other specialist legal fields have, in certain industries, become core competencies for in-house lawyers. Going forward, in-house practitioners will need to anticipate the key emerging issues for their organisations and judge carefully where they focus their skills as the tide of new business opportunities ebbs and flows.

As in-house counsel battled for more recognition and respect in the early years, they necessarily needed to differentiate themselves to some extent from their external colleagues. In practical terms, that differentiation often involved separating the client's legal work into mutually exclusive areas of practice which were respectively reserved to the in-house or the external legal teams. In many cases, these work divisions were rigidly enforced in order to optimise perceived cost advantages. Sometimes, however, the emphasis on cost savings came at the expense of quality or failed to take advantage of the inherent synergies that a combined in-house/ external legal team could have delivered at lower blended cost.

A key challenge for future generations of in-house lawyers will be to develop the capacity to continuously adapt and utilise the 'make or buy' decision in imaginative ways that truly take advantage of the strengths and weaknesses of respective in-house and external legal teams while fully utilising their inherent synergies. In the end, in-house counsel retain the overall responsibility for the provision of legal services to the client, including responsibility for its quality and cost. It remains a matter of judgment how best to meet that need.

The growth of the in-house segment of the legal profession in Australia over recent years was mirrored by a similar development in other countries around the world. Unsurprisingly, that growth has prompted the establishment of many new in-house lawyer member organisations similar to ACLA. With its origins in the 1960's, ACLA was one of the first fully dedicated in-house lawyer member organisations to be established. Another important challenge for tomorrow's in-house counsel will be to develop their member organisations into influential, internationally networked, professional bodies that speak out fearlessly on issues of relevance to in-house counsel and their clients around the world.

Challenges facing the profession

The legal profession in Australia consists mainly of large numbers of small and medium-sized legal practices located in the cities and suburbs. Law societies and other bodies that represent the legal profession broadly reflect that constituency.

However, the interests of the big end of town — major corporations and government — are largely served by a small number of very large international law firms, a few medium- sized general practices and some niche players. The large firms and practices traditionally provided (and still do) most of the usually quite junior practitioners who move in-house.

However, when in-house practice suddenly grew so rapidly in recent years, what had always been a manageable process of transition suddenly became a major problem. Not only were larger numbers of lawyers moving in-house and taking valuable law firm knowledge with them, but in-house practice was suddenly absorbing mid-level lawyers and even senior partners.

At about the same time, a growing number of Australian lawyers found that they could earn good money practising in England while enjoying the sights of Europe. What became known as the 'Magic Circle' of major United Kingdom law firms (and later, their United States 'White Shoe' competitors) came to realise that they could employ young, hard-working Australian lawyers and get good value for their money. As those firms grew and expanded around the world, they offered fascinating new and very well paid job opportunities for travelling young Australian lawyers in places as far afield as Shanghai, Dubai, Hong Kong, New York and Berlin. Australia's law firms suddenly found that retaining staff had become a critical issue.

In a bid to stem the flow of young talent to in-house and overseas positions, Australia's Big Six law firms upped the ante considerably and began to offer top young lawyers first rate, flexible employment packages that competed very successfully with those offered by corporations and overseas law firms. As well, they offered a range of special incentives for talented young lawyers — especially those destined for partnership — such as sign-on bonuses and performance payments. The firms also paid very significant finders' fees to talent scouts and recruiters and even spotters' fees to those of their own staff members who were able to introduce top talent.

This dramatic change in law firm remuneration structure had many follow-on consequences. The road to partnership within most law firms became longer and tougher for aspiring young lawyers as partner numbers were frozen or cut back. The traditional 'lock-step' approach to partnership, based on seniority and years of service, was abandoned by many firms and a meritocracy was introduced. This entailed longer working hours for all and more competition among colleagues. New pre-partner levels of appointment were introduced and partner support infrastructures were heavily trimmed.

At the same time, law firm life became harder as corporate and government clients moved to rationalise and reduce their reliance on expensive external legal advisers. A range of unpleasant new competitive measures was imposed on firms including beauty parades, panels, relationship agreements and fee-caps. In response, the firms turned to new and imaginative ways to maintain their profitability. These included subscribing to a scheme of capped liability; operational optimisation through mergers and acquisitions; incorporation; the creation of one-stop multidisciplinary practices; and, most recently, by listing on the stock exchange.

Fast-forward to today and we find that staff attraction and retention has become an issue not just for the law firms but for the in-house profession as well. With law firms again growing and expanding their partner numbers in the new competitive environment of the legal business, it has become very much harder for all branches of the profession to find and retain good lawyers. Talented in-house lawyers are now keenly sought for roles in Australian law firms and overseas law firms as well as corporations (who increasingly place them in senior line-management functions). What went around has come around.

A key challenge to the in-house profession in future years is going to be to attract and retain good people. In a few years, when the current baby-boomer generation of general counsel gives way to its Generation X successors, it will be fascinating to watch how the new guys on the block try to meet this challenge. The seemingly greater upward mobility and changed personal commitment now evident in all branches of the legal workplace will not make it any easier.

But there are other challenges facing the legal profession too. Perhaps the most significant of them is a challenge to its standing as a true 'profession'. In a mercantilist age, this is a challenge which involves the vexed issues of how to maintain standards and ensure proper levels of education. As we know, the pursuit of high standards of professional and ethical conduct is a hallmark of every true profession. Real professions must have the interests of the wider community at heart and operate selflessly without bringing themselves into disrepute.

In the corporate and government sectors of the legal profession, the rising demand for commercially-oriented legal advice and the pressures on turn-around times and costs can put the independence and integrity of its practising lawyers in jeopardy. In the in-house context, where the lawyer serves one master in two very different capacities — as employee and counsel — those pressures are greatly compounded. Maintaining professional standards and independence in an increasingly tough and unforgiving business environment is perhaps the greatest single challenge that the in-house profession will face in coming years.

As Australia moves glacially towards the establishment of a nationally regulated legal services market, the in-house sector is in a unique position to help shape its own destiny. It has the opportunity to ensure that the new regulatory regime properly takes account of its newly acquired stature and the particularities of its practice. As part of this endeavour, the in-house profession can and must move to secure proper recognition from, and appropriate representation on, whatever national body is eventually charged with the oversight of the new system. Perhaps the recent introduction of a Graduate Diploma of In-house Legal Practice by the College of Law, specifically designed for new and transitioning in-house lawyers, as well as the establishment by ACLA of a National Mentoring

Program for young in-house practitioners around Australia, are positive early indicators that the in-house profession is seizing this opportunity. It is an opportunity that the in-house legal profession must not miss.

The challenges of practising in-house

Having said that *the* critical professional challenge now facing in-house lawyers in Australia is the challenge of maintaining independence, it is important to remember that, as counsel, our paramount duties are to the court and to our client. The question is whether tomorrow's business ethic will continue to permit the degree of real independence that in-house lawyers need in order to be able to give dispassionate, fearless legal advice.

As in-house practice becomes increasingly more project oriented, more international and more inter-disciplinary, management will inevitably tend to regard in-house legal advisers as business people bringing legal expertise to the table rather than as lawyers operating within a business. If in-house counsel fail to make, maintain and manage the distinctions between the different capacities in which they act, the consequences could be serious. A lawyer not acting in a legal capacity cannot claim standing before the courts and cannot attract client legal privilege. Furthermore, when counsel does not act as counsel there are potential issues around professional indemnity insurance and whether or not the indemnity policy will respond. As well, in-house lawyers, like other professionals, are now being asked to accept greater individual accountability (and even liability) for the advice they give. In these circumstances, it is essential that they ensure their advice is properly demarcated.

Some American commentators suggest that the world of legal services is flattening — that tasks are being unbundled and lower-level work outsourced, often to lower-wage countries.[4] This is a trend that could also affect the in-house profession. The fact is that some substitutable services are already being moved offshore to take advantage of lower cost. If that practice grows, it will have significant consequences for workload and staffing within Australian legal departments.

The management and delivery of legal services in the in-house context have already been greatly complicated by globalisation and the consequent need to set appropriate legal and ethical standards that ensure uniformity across international borders. The advent of the structured cross-border outsourcing of legal and legal process services will present yet another complex dimension to this tough professional challenge.

In the public sector, professional obligations often flow from the identity of the client. While the Crown is indivisible, government agencies are often statutory bodies with their own independent legal personalities. As well, government departments and agencies may have separate rights and responsibilities which can often put them at odds with each other. Government departments and agencies are required to conduct themselves as model litigants and lawyers acting for them must assist them to meet their obligations. In-house counsel who are Commonwealth public servants are also required to uphold the principle that the public service is openly accountable to the Australian public and similar principles apply in most states and territories.

As cost and commercial pressures on governments increase and government entities and agencies continue to be spun off and corporatised, lawyers in government agencies will inevitably face new and more complex professional issues. The challenge for them, as for their colleagues in the corporate sector, will be to adapt and change with the terrain, while still maintaining their professionalism.

The nature of in-house practice, both government and corporate, has changed dramatically over the years. From writing up contracts and drafting opinions, in-house lawyers have moved decisively upstream. They now add value at the highest strategic levels. Today's in-house lawyers also often combine multiple roles and offer integrated advice drawn from many sources in real time. Increasingly, in-house lawyers brief the bar directly or appear themselves in court or in tribunals in order to advocate for their clients. Those who do all this successfully keep their business and legal skills finely-honed. They stay abreast of new developments in the law, in legal practice and in the risk profiles of their businesses. This enables them to add measurable value to their client's decision-making processes.

The challenge for the future, however, will be to identify new ways to stay ahead of developments and anticipate future risks while retaining the necessary degree of independence and professionalism. As the business terrain continues to change, in-house lawyers have to be able to help their clients avoid risk and advance their businesses. Staying ahead of the game will be one of the greatest tests of the newly come of age in-house profession.

The business challenge

The business environment within which all these challenges to our profession are framed is not static. The previous decade was one of low interest rates and continuous economic growth tempered somewhat by drought and occasional mismanagement. A skills shortage and low unemployment rates kept wages high while days lost to industrial stoppages dropped to an all-time low. In this positive business environment, it was not surprising that the in-house legal profession thrived. There were jobs aplenty and plenty of applicants for them. The attitude towards in-house lawyers shifted quite significantly in their favour and the pressure that had always been on them to continuously demonstrate their value and contain legal costs, eased.[5] On the other hand, the legislative fall-out from the rise of international terrorism and the big United States and Australian corporate collapses of some years ago vastly complicated their lives. A recent, perhaps short-lived, flood of private equity-financed acquisitions further changed the complexion of the corporate scene.

What then of the future?

Many Australian economists now predict that the coming years will bring an economic slowdown and increasing interest rates — as witnessed in the United States sub-prime crisis and the consequent credit squeeze worldwide. They note that the boom of past years was resources led and depended largely on a voracious, primarily Chinese, appetite for Australian raw materials. But China is now developing other sources of supply and Australia may struggle to remain cost-competitive. The recent change of government in Australia is likely to lead the country towards a greener, more consultative industrial approach which may further impact on its competitiveness. In addition, there are serious questions to be answered around issues such as oil supply, global warming and currency values. For Australian business and its legal advisers, it seems that decision making in uncertainty will continue to be the norm.

If economic growth does slow down we must once again expect closer attention to be paid to costs. But what can be done? Australia's in-house lawyers already work an average of 50 hours a week,[6] so working longer to reduce unit costs is not a real option. One solution may be to work smarter rather than longer. By re-examining the structure of their client's work processes, it might be possible for in-house lawyers to make more informed decisions about which jobs can or should be automated, outsourced or performed in-house. Within each of these categories there is scope for further measures which can be taken to minimise cost and produce value.

The first challenge, however, will be to find and retain the quality staff needed to undertake that analysis, to obtain buy-in and apply the solutions. As the push to globalise tends more towards bilateral, defensive arrangements, and as hyper-competition cools within the new higher-interest-rates economic environment, in-house counsel will again face the challenge of adapting their practices to a new business landscape. In the new environment, the percentage of legal work conducted in-house could well plateau, especially if headcount once again emerges as the paramount measure of cost — as it once was.

For government lawyers, the future of in-house legal practice may well depend more on the direction of policy reform in the area of procurement of government legal services and how that impacts on the in-house/external work balance. With some exceptions, government legal work has been open for competition for over 10 years. Yet, in that time, the government in-house segment has grown substantially faster. For example, between 2000 and 2004, there was a 29% increase in the number of government lawyers employed in New South Wales.[7] As well, despite much publicity about the high level of government expenditure on legal services, that expenditure continues to rise. So, with the business of government becoming more and more complex and the growth in its legal expenditure continuing, there do not appear to be any huge clouds gathering over the future of in-house government practice in Australia.

In-house lawyers are key point-persons in both corporations and government. They are looked to by management, regulatory authorities and the broader community as the people who can identify legal risk and ensure that appropriate governance and compliance mechanisms are in place. However, the in-house lawyers' role in corporate governance is increasingly under the spotlight. As both professional lawyer and company officer, the in-house legal practitioner is certainly in a position to promote good corporate practice and responsible conduct and to help the client develop an appropriate governance model. These tasks draw on the lawyer's specific knowledge of applicable legal requirements as well as on his or her judgment. It entails helping to ensure that appropriate and reliable internal information flows are in place and that external disclosures to regulators and other third parties are accurate and transparent. But there is a worrying and growing trend emerging worldwide in this area towards the imposition of specific legal responsibilities and obligations on in-house counsel; for example, by the long-arm provisions of the United States Sarbanes-Oxley Act (largely adopted in Australia through CLERP 9).

In Australia too, the Corporations Act 2001 (Cth) imposes specific obligations of care on corporate officers. Since the 2004 decision in *ASIC v Vines* (2005) 55 ACSR 617 it has become clear that professionals such as in-house lawyers are expected to discharge those responsibilities to a level that is commensurate with the expertise for which they were appointed. In addition, there are other specific statutes which impose legal consequences for inaccurate, misleading or deceptive communications, many of which impinge on in-house counsel.

The input of in-house lawyers to the design and oversight of governance, compliance and disclosure mechanisms is essential in modern corporations and government, but it is increasingly the subject of penalties and personal risk. In-house counsel are already often made mandatory whistleblowers and/or star witnesses in cases of corporate failure. Yet, it seems likely that as in-house lawyers move to adopt codes of conduct and other policies and processes that ensure transparency and up-the-ladder reporting, their responsibilities and potential exposures will further escalate. This is particularly so as a broader range of interest groups, competitors and shareholders explore new ways to hold corporate management to account.

A key challenge for the future will be to ensure that in-house counsel can discharge their obligations appropriately while avoiding undue personal liability. This can include self-defence measures such as indemnities, insurance and appropriate management of personal assets.

Whither in-house practice?

A worrying concern for all Australian and many overseas in-house lawyers as we move on into the next business phase is that in-house practice is currently facing some specific professional challenges. Already, some years ago, the European Court of Justice removed the right of European in-house counsel to claim client legal privilege on behalf of their clients. It did this on the ground that, as employees, in-house lawyers were not sufficiently independent from their clients to be able to claim privilege.

In Australia, in-house lawyers have fortunately always been treated, at least at law, as full members of the legal profession. In this respect, there has been no distinction made between in-house counsel and external counsel. However, some are now questioning that assumption. Last year, the Commonwealth Attorney-General asked the ALRC to investigate and report on whether client legal privilege should be modified or abrogated. Importantly, the inquiry encompassed whether in-house counsel should be entitled to continue to claim privilege for their clients, and whether corporations should still have the benefit of client legal privilege. While the ALRC eventually recommended no changes in these respects, the government has yet to consider their report and the courts, of course, remain free to make their own findings. Needless to say, these important questions go to the very heart of in-house practice and are being taken very seriously by its practitioners.

The abrogation of privilege in the case of corporations would jeopardise the possibility of full and frank communications between corporate officers and their legal advisers and would undermine legal input into corporate decision-making. Should the right to claim client legal privilege on behalf of their clients be lost to in-house counsel it would clearly disadvantage those very lawyers who are closest to the business in their day-to-day activities, and best placed to identify areas of potential legal risk and advise accordingly.[8] The abrogation of privilege for in-house lawyers could swing the in-house/external work balance more in favour of external law firms, with consequent cost implications for all corporate and government clients.

Another concern for in-house lawyers is the move to introduce the National Legal Profession Model Bill and Model Regulations for the regulation of a national Australian legal profession.[9] In reality, this laudable initiative has unfortunately created a number of specific problems for in-house lawyers, who were largely overlooked during the drafting process.

While the Model Bill and Model Regulations does constitute a significant step towards the establishment of national regulation of the legal profession, regrettably, both it and the state and territory legislation which has so far implemented it, have left much to be desired. For example, despite ACLA's view that for a range of reasons it would be desirable for all Australian corporate and government solicitors to hold practising certificates, the Model Bill and Model Regulations does not implement that requirement. On the other hand, it does require newly admitted practitioners who do take out practising certificates to be supervised for a period of time before they can qualify for an unrestricted certificate. As in-house lawyers know, however, it is not actually possible for them to engage in supervised practice while employed by a corporation specifically because of the very narrow definitions that are contained in the Model Bill and Model Regulations itself. This unnecessary and undesirable complication has so far only been addressed piecemeal through a number of state-based exemption arrangements. No one has tackled the real problem — the wording of the Model Bill and Model Regulations.

In addition, the Model Bill and Model Regulations contains a quaint prohibition on the use of the title 'Senior Counsel', which is now to be reserved solely for use by practitioners, typically from the bar, who have been appointed as such. This is despite the long-standing corporate practice of appointing experienced in-house counsel in corporations to positions titled 'Senior Counsel.'

Last but not least, there has been some skirmishing concerning Rule 19.1 of the Model Rules of Professional Conduct.[10] The Model Rules are drafted as policies and guidelines for the national profession. Rule 19.1 arguably would prevent all solicitors, including those practising in-house, from commenting publicly on legal proceedings in which they are involved. Following loud protests, the Law Council of Australia eventually agreed to revisit the scope and operation of that Rule.

The confusion around the Model Bill and Model Regulations and its non-uniform implementation within Australia has been exacerbated for in-house counsel by the ongoing, and apparently uncoordinated, reform campaigns of federal, state and territory governments and national and local law societies. A very high percentage of in-house lawyers still belong to law societies around Australia. This is despite the fact that membership of such bodies is now largely a matter of choice since the licensing and oversight of the profession — including the issue of practising certificates — has been mostly transferred to statutory authorities.

In practice, this means that via the capitation fees which the law societies pay to the Law Council of Australia, a very significant proportion of the council's funding is actually provided by the in-house profession. Furthermore, in-house lawyers in some states and territories, despite their very low-risk profile, continue to be required to contribute to solicitors' fidelity funds and under the Model Bill and Model Regulations, will continue to do so.

These involuntary contributions by the in-house profession to the law societies are unfortunately neither recognised nor rewarded. The in-house profession and ACLA have long pleaded for a national approach to the regulation and oversight of the Australian legal profession. Yet, state governments and law societies have launched a series of uncoordinated local reviews and initiatives involving various aspects of the legal profession — including several matters of concern to the in-house profession — that could better have been dealt with nationally. As an example, the Queensland and Victorian Governments have approved systems of compulsory legal education that differs significantly from the long-standing New South Wales model but which still take little or no account of the special requirements of corporate and government lawyers.

The paucity of concern for the particular interests of the in-house legal profession in Australia is also reflected in the fact that only the law societies of New South Wales and Victoria currently have entrenched positions on their councils for corporate and government lawyers. The Law Council of Australia, the peak organisation for Australia's legal profession (which recently granted a seat on its council to the newly created Large Law Firm Group) has no representation whatsoever from the ranks of in-house counsel.

A major challenge for the in-house profession in coming years will be to overcome these inequities and to ensure that the voice of corporate and government lawyers is heard at all relevant levels of government and the legal profession.

Summary

As is the case in various overseas jurisdictions, the in-house profession in Australia — both government and corporate — has come of age. The future, in terms of job satisfaction and growth seems rosy, at least for the time being. But the economic and business landscape is again changing and in-house lawyers must adapt. Coping with an ever rising workload, staff attraction and retention,[11] and the maintenance of professionalism and independence in a changing world are key challenges for the incoming generation. Other complex dimensions are added by cross-border outsourcing of legal-related services and the need to stay ahead of the game in identifying risk and adding value. For government lawyers, the pressures of commercialisation and the possibility of further reforms to the system of procurement of legal services will provide additional challenges.

As the growing cost of legal services and the rising uncertainty about the economic future resurface as key issues, tomorrow's Australian in-house lawyers face a range of significant professional issues: the possible abrogation of the right to claim privilege; an inconsistent/incomplete national regulatory regime; and a lack of appropriate representation on state and national bodies.

The critical challenge for the in-house profession remains in essence what it always was: to balance the often competing commercial and professional requirements of the role. It is an exciting and demanding challenge and one to which the in-house profession will certainly successfully rise. The in-house legal profession in Australia is presently in great shape. It is the task of the next generation of in-housers to keep it that way.

---

*   The views expressed in this chapter are the individual views of the author and are not necessarily views known to or shared by ACLA.

1   '2006 Profile of the Solicitors of NSW', unpublished report prepared for the Law Society of New South Wales by Urbis Keys Young, Sydney, 2007, p 14.
2   'The Solicitors of NSW in 2015', unpublished report prepared for the Law Society of New South Wales by Urbis Keys Young, Sydney, 2004, p 10.
3   Mahlab Recruitment, 'Survey 2008 — Corporate', in 'Survey 2008', Melbourne and Sydney, 2008, p 8. Available at <http://www.mahlab.com.au> then 'Publications'.
4   David Galbenski, 'The Effects of a Flattening Legal World', *Lumen Legal Newsroom*, April 2007, p 1.
5   Beaton Consulting, 'In-house Law Report 2007', unpublished report prepared for ACLA, Melbourne, 2007, p 3.
6   Mahlab Recruitment, op cit, p 9.
7   'The Solicitors of New South Wales in 2015', op cit, p 37, Table 7.
8   See <http://www.acla.com.au> then 'What's New?', 'June 25, 2007: ACLA makes Submission to ALRC Privilege Inquiry'.
9   For news on the Model Rules Project, see <http://www.lawcouncil.asn.au> then 'National Practice'.
10   For the Model Rules on Professional Conduct, see <http://www.lawcouncil.asn .au> then 'Policies and Guidelines'.
11   Team Factors, *ACLA/CLANZ Legal Department Benchmarking Report 2008*, Wellington, 2008, p 55.

PART 2

Managing Self

2

TRANSITIONING FROM EXTERNAL COUNSEL TO IN-HOUSE COUNSEL

by

Chua Lee Ming[*]

Chua Lee Ming is General Counsel of the Government of Singapore Investment Corporation Pte Ltd (GIC). He holds an LLB from the National University of Singapore, an LLM from Cambridge University and is admitted to practise law in Singapore, England and Wales. Lee Ming previously served in the Singapore judicial service. He later became a litigation partner at Lee & Lee before joining GIC to head its legal department. Lee Ming is also currently Vice-President of the Singapore Corporate Counsel Association.

Introduction

'Conduit', 'retirement job', 'mundane', 'postbox': these are some of the words one used to hear whenever the topic of in-house counsel arose. Traditionally, in-house counsel has been more of an administrator whose primary role has been to instruct external counsel and act as a conduit between external counsel and the management or business people in a company or organisation.

However, be it revolution or evolution, the role of in-house counsel has clearly changed over the last couple of decades. The change may have taken place more rapidly in some jurisdictions than in others. However, what is clear is that today companies increasingly rely on in-house counsel to perform legal work previously outsourced to external counsel and also to take on broader strategic roles within organisations.

Indeed, in recognising the key role played by in-house counsel in settlement negotiations, in a case before the Court of Appeal of Singapore, *Britestone Pte Ltd v Smith & Associates Far East Ltd* [2007] SGCA 47, the court has highlighted (at [66]):

> … it is not essential for legal advice to be invariably sought from external counsel. As long as the advice given is, when objectively viewed, independent, sensible and rational, it will be accorded some weight, regardless of the source. In other words, the identity of the legal adviser is not critical — what is crucial is, instead, whether the legal advice given is indeed prudent, sound and consistent with established legal principles.

It would be fair to say that the in-house counsel community has now earned recognition as the fourth branch of the legal fraternity. The other three branches (at least in the context of Singapore) are private legal practice, judiciary and government legal service, and academia.

Several factors have brought about the increase in reliance on in-house counsel. One obvious reason is the need to manage legal costs. However, in many cases, the reason is simply due to the more complex ways in which companies operate in today's environment of technological advances and increasing globalisation. Legal and regulatory compliance are now major concerns. Transactions are more complicated. The commercial world is highly innovative. In-house counsel will have to navigate the intricacies of the legal world as well as the complexities of the commercial one; legal risks cannot be properly managed without a good appreciation of both. This requires a good appreciation of how law and business work. Clearly, intimate knowledge of a company's structure, business and operations is required, and in-house counsel are the ones who are able to acquire this knowledge.

Equally, there appears to be greater interest in in-house employment positions. One consequence of the enhanced role of in-house counsel and the complex legal work they handle is that in-house positions now offer increasingly challenging legal work. In-house counsel now perform 'real' legal work. In fact, in some cases, in-house positions probably offer a degree of specialisation that may not be easily found in private practice. The broader role of in-house counsel has also led to the lateral development of skills and broader experiences. As a result of the demand for in-house counsel and the broader responsibilities that they now have to bear, the gap between compensation for in-house positions and that of practitioners has also narrowed.

Technological advances and globalisation have also increased the stress on practitioners. Although in-house counsel's work is by no means simple, generally speaking, their work does provide a more balanced lifestyle in many cases. Also, unlike their counterparts in private practice, in-house counsel have a captive client and there is no need to seek or develop clients (although this captive client relationship gives rise to different problems).

Anecdotal evidence shows that the most common reasons for practitioners opting to move in-house are a more balanced lifestyle; the fact that there is no need to look for clients; and the opportunity to work more closely with the business side of an organisation, on transactions. It is no surprise that more and more practitioners are leaving private practice to join the in-house community.

However, it is not always easy for a lawyer from private practice to adapt to life as in-house counsel. The transition requires many adjustments to be made to the way one thinks and works. While it is true that both external and in-house counsel are involved in legal work, the similarity often ends there. One major difference is that an external counsel's focus is on the practice of law, whereas in-house counsel cannot escape from the fact that they are part of their respective business organisations. The focus of in-house counsel must necessarily be on how to help their organisation achieve key business objectives.

This chapter examines the issues that lawyers in private practice are likely to face when they move in-house. Admittedly, some of these issues are not exclusive to in-house counsel; they may be faced by external counsel as well. However, external counsel often either have less problems or have greater flexibility in dealing with these issues due to their independent status *vis-à-vis* the client. The fact that an in-house counsel is an employee of the company does make some of these issues more challenging.

In general, a successful transition requires two things. First, a clear understanding of the realities surrounding and the expectations imposed upon an in-house counsel. Second, there must be certain mindset or behavioural changes which are required in order to meet these realities and expectations. The changes required are at an individual level and to be successful at making such changes self-awareness is key.

Less autonomy, more involvement

One of the key realities for in-house counsel is that external counsel typically enjoy greater autonomy. External counsel deal only with certain appointed representatives of corporate clients. They advise the representative who makes or conveys the company's decisions, and then proceed on the basis of those decisions.

In contrast, in-house counsel are often required to liaise with various different departments and personnel within the business organisation. In many cases, this means having to obtain comments and, in some cases, approval from several persons before proceeding further. External counsel are spared all this; they see only the final decision as conveyed to them. In-house counsel cannot simply wait for instructions — they have to be more pro-active and, if necessary, be the catalyst in getting others in the company to make the requisite decisions.

The higher level of involvement by the in-house counsel in company affairs raises the question of 'Who is the client?'. An external counsel deals with representatives of corporate clients such as a commercial manager or in-house counsel. Such representatives are generally taken to represent the client. In contrast, an in-house counsel has to constantly remember that the client is the company and not any individual employee or officer of that company. In fact, the interests of specific commercial managers, and even the CEO, can sometimes diverge from the interests of the company. Discerning and protecting the real interests of the company then become paramount. This task is often made more difficult because company employees and officers are less likely to draw the distinction between the company and themselves when they consult their in-house counsel.

Similarly, giving advice can be a lot more challenging for in-house counsel where there is possible wrongdoing by the company's employees. The relationship that an in-house counsel has with his or her colleagues in the company is more likely to be closer than that which an external counsel would have. There is the risk, therefore, that the advice of the in-house counsel may be less objective than that of external counsel.

Due to the greater involvement of in-house counsel with others in the organisation, it is important for them to develop the necessary soft skills for dealing with people. They have to understand and manage the different personalities within the company that are important to their areas of work.

The changed relationship with external counsel

Another change facing in-house counsel revolves around the relationship with external counsel. Anecdotes about unreasonable clients are common among all legal practitioners. 'Yesterday' deadlines are standard jokes. Most, if not all, practitioners have had clients giving instructions on Friday afternoon, with the expectation of the complete advice by Monday morning. The usual caricature is that of an external counsel who spends the weekend working while the in-house counsel plays golf. The key point, however, is that the external counsel who moves in-house is now, of course, the client to other external counsel. It is often said (not always in jest) that he or she is now in the enviable position to be that unreasonable client.

Fortunately, it is more often the case that the practitioner who becomes an in-house counsel is in fact sympathetic to the plight of external counsel. The notion that an in-house counsel typically becomes an unreasonable client appears to be mere fodder for jokes among practitioners rather than a depiction of reality. Nevertheless, it is critically important for in-house counsel to understand what the in-house counsel role is *vis-à-vis* external counsel. When external counsel is engaged, it should be because the matter requires specialised expertise which the in-house counsel does not have, or because it is more efficient to outsource the matter. An in-house counsel should then cease to behave as though he or she were still a practitioner handling the matter.

Once external counsel is engaged for whatever reason, the in-house counsel must not continue to supervise the external counsel in the same way that a partner or senior associate in a law firm might supervise a junior lawyer. This means that the in-house counsel must learn to manage the external counsel without examining and checking every little detail of the external counsel's work; the fact is that the work has been outsourced. An in-house counsel who continues to work on the matter as he or she would have done as external counsel is defeating the very purpose of outsourcing.

Having said that, lawyers who move in-house often find it difficult to refrain from scrutinising the details of external counsel's work. In some respect, this is understandable; psychologically one tends to find greater comfort in staying within one's comfort zone. The practitioner who becomes an in-house counsel might even view the external counsel as a 'threat' leading to efforts being made to show that the in-house counsel is better than the external counsel. This is of course a misconception of what the in-house counsel role should be. In-house counsel must understand and realise that his or her role is not to duplicate the work of, but to manage, external counsel. This includes assessing external counsel's work and deciding whether or not to continue using that counsel for current and future matters. If that work is unprofessional, then the external counsel should no longer be used.

Being 'commercial'

A key expectation imposed on all lawyers advising corporate clients on commercial matters is that they must be commercially-minded. Indeed, in-house counsel are expected to be even more commercially-minded then their practitioner counterparts. But what does being 'commercially-minded' mean?

It does not merely mean being able to understand the business, financial analysis or business considerations in respect to a particular company or transaction. Being commercially-minded is an attitude. It refers to the desire to complete a deal undeterred by obstacles. It is the attitude of determination to find solutions to problems so that a deal can be done. This requires flexibility, creativity and lateral thinking. It means asking questions such as 'Are there alternative ways to achieve a particular objective without running foul of laws?', and 'Is there a different way to draft a particular clause so that it meets the concerns of all parties?'. Saying 'no', 'it cannot be done' or 'it has to be done this way' is easy. Being commercially-minded refers to the determined attitude of finding a way to enable a transaction to proceed, with resort to saying 'no' only after all avenues and possibilities have been explored and found wanting.

Take, for example, negotiations on an agreement. If an amendment proposed by the opposing side is not acceptable, in-house counsel must always look for alternative ways to achieve the objective of the clause instead of simply reverting to the original language and rejecting the proposed amendment outright. In-house counsel must examine what are the interests of the company that have to be protected by the clause in question. They should then explore other ways of re-drafting the clause so as to achieve this objective, while at the same time addressing the opposing party's concerns over the original language. This is so even if in-house counsel feel strongly that the opposing party's concerns are unfounded. Sticking resolutely to one's position on the ground that 'this is what the law states' is being legalistic (at best), unrealistic and impractical.

Another example of being commercially-minded is concerned with what may be referred to as 'being right' or 'getting it right'. An in-house counsel has to be able to look at the broader picture and not remain focused on making sure that every detail or legal principle is correctly stated. As in-house counsel, one has to be prepared to proceed even if one feels that a point in contention is doubtful or even wrong, if, on proper analysis, the inclusion of the wrong point, drafting or assumption of principle of law would have no or minimal adverse effect on the company. This is a decision which the in-house counsel (not the external counsel) has to make. An external counsel who has been in the habit of leaving this decision to his or her client (or the client's in-house counsel) must make that mental switch once the move in-house has been made and be prepared to make that decision independently.

The flip side to being more commercial is the temptation to be less 'legal'. One specific factor which can lead in-house counsel to lose some of their legal skills is the failure to keep up-to-date with developments in the law. To counter this, they must constantly remind themselves to stay updated; client updates from law firms are one good way to keep in touch with developments in the law.

In-house counsel as insider

Another important reality to acknowledge is that an in-house counsel is an insider. Employees of a company tend not to treat in-house counsel the same way as they treat external counsel. The reason is perhaps a psychological one: an in-house counsel is seen as a fellow employee and a colleague.

This has both advantages and disadvantages. Employees are more likely to open up to in-house counsel than to external counsel. However, in-house counsel face greater pressure to provide answers immediately, whereas external counsel are more likely to be given time to carry out research and to analyse the issues. In-house counsel who repeatedly ask for time to consult external counsel, or to check the law, are not likely to earn a great deal of respect from their business colleagues. In-house counsel are expected to stay on top of what is relevant to, or affects, the company.

External counsel are also less likely to be concerned over who in the company might be affected or feel criticised by their advice. On the contrary, they are expected to tell the company if any part of the company's processes or practices is wrong and needs rectification; any such criticism from external counsel is more readily accepted. In contrast, in-house counsel are regarded as company employees. While their constructive criticism is expected, it is still harder for in-house counsel to criticise some parts of the company or their colleagues. In-house counsel have to be more conscious of how their advice affects their colleagues. After all, they have to continue working with those colleagues in the future.

As an insider, the in-house counsel is expected to understand all aspects of the company well. There is sometimes an expectation (albeit, not always a very reasonable one) that an in-house counsel should also know about all legal systems and laws that are relevant to the company's activities. For example, where the company operates in common and civil law jurisdictions, the in-house counsel is likely to be expected to be fairly conversant with both legal systems. Yet, there would be ready acceptance of the limitations to the expertise of an external counsel.

In-house counsel are also expected to understand at least the fundamentals of all aspects of the company's business, processes and operations. They need to know how to think like their business colleagues and to understand the legal needs of the company. They must develop the ability to identify potential legal issues for the company and to help the company avoid such legal problems. In contrast, external counsel are more readily forgiven for not understanding the company quite as well.

Hence, the burden on in-house counsel in this respect is clearly far greater when compared to external counsel. In-house counsel cannot say 'I did not know about this aspect of the company's business or operations'. In fact, the main advantage they have over external counsel is their more intimate knowledge of the company's business and operations. For this reason, in-house counsel must expect to learn various non-legal matters. The law may be central to external counsel and they may also be forgiven for thinking that business revolves around the law. In-house counsel, on the other hand, must quickly come to terms with the fact that the law is not at the centre of the business universe. They must view the law from the perspective of business, not business from the perspective of the law.

The fact that an in-house counsel is an insider often reduces the opportunity for him or her to bounce legal arguments off other lawyers. Of course, if an in-house legal team is large and has a number of in-house counsel, then there are opportunities to discuss legal issues with fellow in-house counsel. Otherwise, those who work as the sole legal adviser for a company tend to find that daily work is bereft of opportunities to discuss legal issues with other lawyers. Such opportunities tend to be more readily available in the context of a law firm than within an in-house legal department.

Recommending or making decisions?

One of the key mindset changes required in the transition to an in-house role revolves around decision-making. An external counsel acts as an adviser to the company; advising the company on the latter's obligations, liabilities, exposures etc. It is then left to the company to make the necessary decisions or to take steps to implement the external counsel's advice.

In contrast, an in-house counsel is usually required to assess the legal risks and to make decisions, or at least take a certain position, and then make recommendations to senior management or the board. The in-house counsel must understand the need to go beyond analysing risks and now take some risks. Hence, an in-house counsel needs to be mentally prepared to take on the challenge of making decisions on legal risks. A decision to proceed carries with it the responsibility for a potential wrong assessment of the extent, seriousness or probability of the associated legal risks. On the other hand, a decision not to proceed usually means having to deal with unhappy business people who are being denied the potential benefits flowing from a proposed transaction.

In making or recommending decisions, in-house counsel should be mindful that in many jurisdictions the communications between them and other company employees can be protected by legal privilege. However, even where legal privilege does apply, it is widely accepted that it applies only to communications with in-house counsel in their capacity as legal advisers.

In-house counsel invariably wear many hats within the company and perform many functions which have little to do with giving legal advice. It is important that in-house counsel are always aware of the multiple hats that they wear. They should ensure that the legal privilege attached to their communications in their capacity as legal advisers is not unwittingly lost or waived as a result of their non-legal functions.

More management, supervision and responsibility

An in-house counsel also needs to be prepared to exercise more managerial functions than an external counsel would. The latter would have little or no concern over a company's corporate policies unless specifically asked to review or draft them. In-house counsel, on the other hand, would invariably be involved in formulating policies. These may have very little to do with the law, and the practitioner who goes in-house must be prepared to step outside his or her comfort zone.

In a similar vein, an in-house counsel is also expected to act as a watchdog over the company's corporate governance. It is incumbent upon in-house counsel to see that steps are taken to rectify weaknesses and address legal risks. It also follows that an in-house counsel must expect to face far greater pressure and calls for accountability whenever the company encounters any legal trouble; he or she will be 'in the thick of things' whenever trouble strikes. In contrast, external counsel is at least one step removed from being in the eye of the storm.

One further area of responsibility faced by in-house counsel is that of managing costs. The reality is that, for many lawyers, moving from private practice to an in-house position means a transition from being a fee-earner to a cost centre. An external counsel is a fee-earner in the law firm in which he or she practises. In contrast, an in-house counsel is generally viewed by the company and his or her colleagues as a cost centre. Hence, practitioners who move in-house have to learn to deal with the change from being one who brings home the bacon to being one who consumes the bacon.

Conclusion

As can be seen from this chapter, there are a multitude of issues which an external counsel has to be aware of and deal with when the transition to in-house is made. Generally, these have to do with two things: the differences between the role and responsibilities of an in-house counsel compared to those of an external counsel; and the level of self-awareness required regarding the changes that need to be made to the way an in-house counsel thinks and approaches his or her work.

Traditionalist lawyers whose minds are preoccupied with the law will probably find the transition to in-house counsel very challenging. In fact, they may find being in-house not quite their cup of tea. On the other hand, lawyers who see their own legal training as a tool to be used in analysing problems and finding innovative solutions will derive immense satisfaction from being in-house counsel. With the appropriate adjustments being made in these two spheres, life as in-house counsel can be most rewarding.

---

*   The author is writing in his personal capacity; all views expressed in this chapter are his own and do not represent views of either the GIC or the Singapore Corporate Counsel Association.

3

MANAGING IN-HOUSE COUNSEL WORKLOAD

by

Benny Tabalujan

Benny Tabalujan has worked in Melbourne, Singapore and Hong Kong as a lawyer, educator and consultant. Through IKD, he has designed and delivered professional development programs for and consulted to in-house legal teams on a range of topics including: ethics, governance and compliance, performance measurement and workload management. Benny has degrees in economics and law from Monash University and a PhD from the University of Melbourne. In addition to his work with IKD, Benny is an adjunct faculty at Melbourne Law School and Melbourne Business School, University of Melbourne, where he teaches in the LLM and MBA programs.

Introduction

According to the *ACLA/CLANZ Legal Department Benchmarking Report 2008*, managing workload and time pressure is 'the single most pressing issue' facing in-house counsel.[1] This finding — which is based on data from legal teams in over 125 organisations throughout Australia and New Zealand — is consistent with anecdotal evidence from my own consulting work with in-house legal teams.

Although among some lawyers there is still a perception that in-house counsel generally work less than their private practice counterparts, in many cases this is not borne out by reality. The report reveals that around 1 in 4 in-house counsel work more than 50 hours per week, with those in small legal teams and those in large corporates (those with $1 billion or more in annual revenues) experiencing a higher likelihood of longer working hours.[2] Public sector legal teams do not fare much better. While there is a greater likelihood that they work less hours than their private sector counterparts, the data indicates that 75% of public sector in-house counsel still work between 41–60 hours in a typical work week.[3]

Heavy workloads and long working hours thus appear to be challenges facing most in-house counsel, regardless of whether they are in the public or private sector. It seems to be an increasingly dominant feature of the role. My own consulting work with legal teams suggests that the failure to manage workload effectively can create negative ripple effects on other in-house legal functions, ranging from the inability to retain good lawyers to a lack of strategic positioning and value creation for the organisation.

In order to facilitate better workload management among in-house counsel, this chapter will analyse what in-house counsel workload is all about and how it can be more effectively handled. Before doing so, there is one caveat. No two in-house counsel roles are identical. For that reason alone, the workload issues facing in-house counsel come in a variety of guises. Having said that, there are some common themes which can be found in many of these roles; it is these that I wish to focus on.

Accordingly, this chapter will discuss what in-house counsel work is all about, describe how some have chosen to manage it, and then provide some tools which may be able to assist others to tackle specific workload challenges. In doing so, this chapter is unlikely to contain much that is new. Nevertheless, I hope that this brief discussion will, to some degree, shed some light on the workload burden of in-house counsel and, by doing so, perhaps lighten it a little.

What is in-house counsel work?

It is useful to begin by describing the nature of in-house counsel work. Through my consulting work with in-house counsel, it is clear that their work covers a broad scope. Indeed, the smaller the legal team, the more variety of work which comes to the in-house counsel. Someone who is a one-person general counsel and company secretary has to deal with a variety of tasks. These can range from preparation and filing of company secretarial documents to drafting, negotiating and managing the gamut of contracts required to facilitate business transactions. Those working in larger legal teams are more likely to be able to specialise in certain types of legal work.

Where there is more than one person in the in-house legal team, I have found it useful to describe in-house counsel workload by using the simple diagram depicted in Figure 3.1. This diagram postulates that each in-house counsel at the core must possess highly developed technical or legal skills. These include basic skills such as legal analysis, statutory interpretation, drafting and negotiation.

Figure 3.1: What in-house counsel work is all about

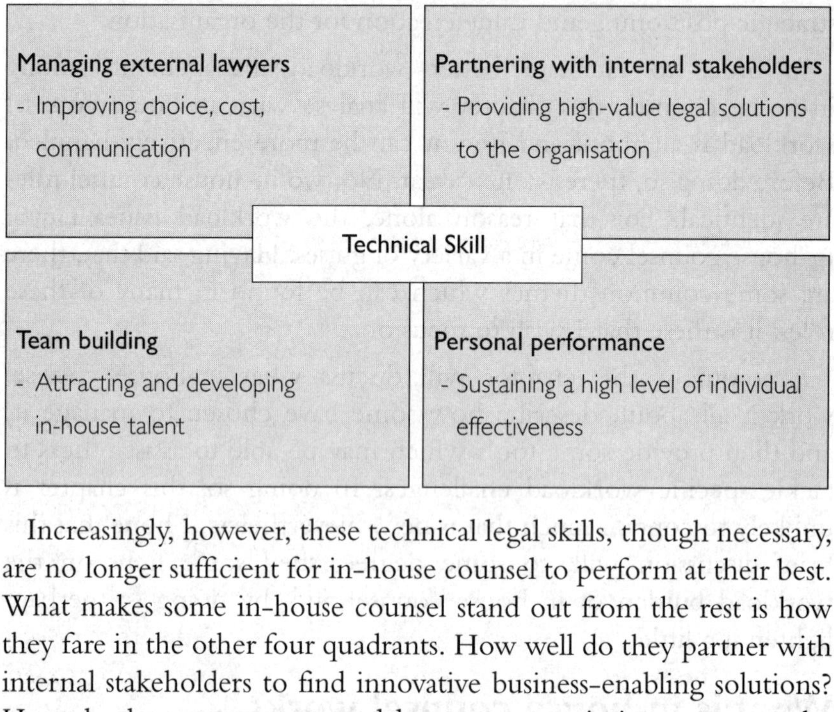

Managing external lawyers	Partnering with internal stakeholders
- Improving choice, cost, communication	- Providing high-value legal solutions to the organisation
Technical Skill	
Team building	Personal performance
- Attracting and developing in-house talent	- Sustaining a high level of individual effectiveness

Increasingly, however, these technical legal skills, though necessary, are no longer sufficient for in-house counsel to perform at their best. What makes some in-house counsel stand out from the rest is how they fare in the other four quadrants. How well do they partner with internal stakeholders to find innovative business–enabling solutions? How do they manage external lawyers to maximise returns to the organisation's legal spend? What can they do to improve overall team performance? And how does an in-house counsel continually improve personal performance and sustain high levels of individual effectiveness?

While these questions differ in thrust and topic, they share common themes. Each involves time. Each requires discernment as to what is valuable or necessary as opposed to what is low value or superfluous. Each requires consistent and, at times, courageous decision making in order to generate positive results. What follows below are suggestions as to how to deal with these key issues. Most of them germinated as ideas in the course of facilitating workshops and dialogues with in-house counsel on specific workload issues.

For ease of understanding I have grouped these suggestions under two headings. The first is 'Identifying valuable work': why identifying high-value work is important and how this can be undertaken. The second, 'Doing the valuable work', focuses on how the high-value work can be performed once it has been identified. These two basic steps, in my mind, sum up the key challenges of managing in-house counsel workload.

Identifying valuable work

The first key challenge facing an in-house legal team is how to identify what is high-value work — that is, work which makes a clear positive impact to the organisation. Too often in-house counsel spend most of their time undertaking lower value work, performing tasks reactively, fighting fires and dealing with a constant stream of requests.

Those who face this particular challenge in their workplaces can begin to tackle the issue by undertaking an assessment of their workflow. A workflow assessment helps to identify business-critical and high-value work. From there, it is possible to create or modify a workflow process which sieves minor matters from significant items. Minor or routine work can be dealt with separately.

For example, a legal team may find that one of its in-house counsel is spending an inordinate amount of time on low impact employment law issues. Instead, these can be briefed out to an appropriate second or third tier law firm at negotiated fee rates. If so, then the in-house counsel has additional time which can be devoted to matters which have greater strategic impact for the organisation. Or, another in-house counsel may spend several hours each week vetting confidentiality agreements. One solution is for standard templates to be created and relevant staff in business units trained to use them. In-house counsel should only be consulted when dealing with more complex variations — which, by definition, constitute higher-value work.

Figure 3.2: Workflow model

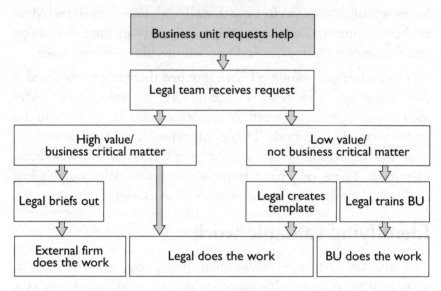

Figure 3.3: Another workflow model

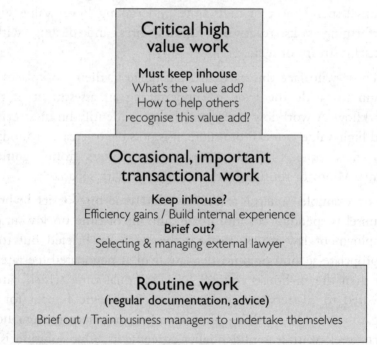

Figure 3.2 depicts a sample workflow model for in-house counsel. This model rejects the notion that in-house counsel should indiscriminately fulfil all work requests made by business units. Instead, under this model, a legal team is still able to be responsive

to requests from business units, but now they are more discerning as to what high-value work will be undertaken by in-house counsel and how other work will be dealt with. Similarly, Figure 3.3 offers another perspective as to how workflow priorities can be determined by in-house counsel. Both models emphasise the importance of identifying what constitutes high-value work within an organisation.

How then do in-house counsel decide as to what constitutes high-value work? The answer depends on the context. Each in-house counsel is employed to help an organisation achieve its aims. For that reason, from the first day of employment the organisation has expectations as to what the in-house counsel can and should contribute. Later, as the in-house counsel learns more about the organisation and its activities, these expectations morph and grow. They often include an expectation that in-house counsel will keep abreast of changes in the legal environment and take pro-active steps to advise the organisation accordingly.

In other words, the expectations upon in-house counsel typically include not only completion of specific work assignments, but also the dynamic task of adjusting their work scope. They have to do the work as well as decide what work has to be done.

Within a legal team and similarly in the case of an individual in-house counsel, expectations and priorities are likely to change over time. A recently appointed general counsel who has to create a legal team from scratch may focus the first six months on team building at the expense of improving the management of external lawyers. On the other hand, a senior counsel hired to tackle a few on-going high-risk transactions may be expected to devote the bulk of his or her time to transactional work with a high level of individual effectiveness. Going back to Figure 3.1, this means that the time and effort spent on each of the four quadrants are not necessarily equal or static.

The key in all this is that there must be a clear understanding as to what expectations are required of the in-house counsel at each point in time. These expectations set the direction of work. The daily tasks are then geared towards achieving those results. If a particular task that day does not contribute to those results, then it does not have to be done. It can simply be deleted or ignored.

For the in-house counsel, understanding what the organisation expects of them is a foundational step. Once these expectations are clear, in-house counsel work should be aligned with and structured to meet these expectations. The great management writer Peter Drucker explained it this way around four decades ago.[4] He was discussing the role of business executives, but he could just as easily have been describing the role of in-house counsel today:

> Effective executives focus on outward contribution. They gear their efforts to results rather than to work. They start out with the question, 'What results are expected of me?' rather than with the work to be done, let alone with its techniques and tools ... Effective executives concentrate on the few major areas where superior performance will produce outstanding results. They force themselves to set priorities and stay with their priority decisions. They know they have no choice but to do first things first and second things not at all. The alternative is to get nothing done.

This process of sifting high-value from low-value work is not to be confused with time management, which we will discuss a little later in the chapter. At this stage, it is important to simply point out that identifying high-value work is part of a broader concept of workload management — and that this is beyond time management. Paraphrasing Stephen Covey, workload management is more about scheduling our priorities than it is prioritising our schedules; it is more about the compass than the clock.[5] Whereas time management focuses on how to maximise the number of tasks done within an hour, workload management is about asking what tasks are important, regardless of whether it will take one hour or one week to complete. In this sense, workload management is to time management what strategy is to tactics.

Doing the valuable work

Once the high-value work expected of an in-house counsel has been identified, the next step is to do it. For many, this is easier said than done. One common hurdle is that the contemporary workplace is incredibly complex. More often than not, there are numerous items competing for the attention of in-house counsel.[6]

Competing requests, unexpected crises, corporate restructurings and legislative or regulatory reforms are just some of the complexities which can dog in-house counsel who are trying to get their high-value work done. Many, though not all, of these complexities appear as interruptions. Some are foreseeable; others are not.

The effective in-house counsel has to develop skills or habits to cope with these complexities and still perform their high-value work.[7] Fortunately, it appears that these skills and habits can be learnt because they are rooted in self-discipline and practice. Several of these skills and habits are based on conventional time management concepts and they are discussed below.

Distinguish the important from the urgent

The first skill which can help in-house counsel fulfil their commitment to perform high-value work is to categorise tasks using the urgent/important matrix. Popularised by Stephen Covey,[8] this matrix provides a simple yet effective way for in-house counsel to distinguish what tasks are truly important in terms of what is expected of them. (Needless to say, these expectations should contribute in a tangible way to achieving the strategic goals of the organisation.) Once this is clear, then it becomes easier to evaluate each task, allocate them to one of the four quadrants in the matrix, and decide whether they should be done or simply set aside.

Figure 3.4: The important/urgent matrix

	Urgent	Not Urgent
Important	**Quadrant 1** - Crises - Pressing problems - Some deadline-driven projects	**Quadrant 2** - Planning, preparing, organising - Improving relationships - Recognising new opportunities - Raising productive capacity
Not Important	**Quadrant 3** - Interruptions - Fluff calls and meetings - Some deadline-driven projects	**Quadrant 4** - Trivia - Email spam - Other time wasters

Source: adapted from Stephen Covey, *The 7 Habits of Highly Effective People* (1990)

In reality, many in-house counsel spend an inordinate amount of time and energy in Q1 and Q3. They spend too little time in Q2. The result is a reactive, ever-busy work style. In contrast, in-house counsel who have developed the habit of sifting the important from the urgent will usually spend the bulk of their time in Q1 and Q2. For example, one in-house counsel pointed out that Q2 activities like relationship-building coffee chats with internal stakeholders may not be urgent, but can be very important. Why? Simply because with better relationships, artificial deadlines go away.

Other important Q2 activities which in-house counsel have found to be especially useful include:

- scheduling thinking time;
- preparing for critical communications — whether written or oral;
- regularly reflecting on how well one's tasks are aligned with the organisation's strategic goals;
- scanning the external environment and networking with peers in other organisations to see how they perform their roles; and
- undertaking professional development programs to expand their skill set.

Leverage one's circadian rhythms

A second habit which may help in-house counsel perform high-value work is to leverage one's circadian rhythms. Research indicates that human bodies have inbuilt circadian rhythms which can have a significant effect on how attentive we are during different parts of a day.[9] For example, most individuals can be categorised as larks (who are most attentive in the mornings) and owls (who are attentive in the evenings). Further, most people are drowsy after lunch until around mid-afternoon, with larks typically experiencing a deeper afternoon malaise than owls. This afternoon malaise can be overcome by coffee or a 20-minute power nap, but is made worse by alcohol.

Understanding one's circadian rhythms enables peak attention times to be reserved for high-value work. For example, one general counsel I know, being a lark, typically puts aside about two hours each morning to undertake a substantive piece of work requiring creativity, deep analysis, or extensive writing. His practice is not to check his email in the morning. He will do so usually at about 11.00 am after his substantive work is done. During this period, his personal assistant will screen calls and will only put calls through from select individuals, including the CEO. In his case, understanding and leveraging his circadian rhythms has enabled him to be more productive than otherwise.

Create time margins

A third habit for helping in-house counsel perform high-value work is to create time margins. Richard Swenson, a medical doctor, popularised the concept of margins in the mid-1990s.[10] His concept was simple. Margin refers to the amount available beyond what is needed. In an age of overloaded working lives, Swenson exhorts individuals to purposefully create margins of empty time in their calendars. In the same way that margins and white space make a printed page more pleasant to read, time margins create essential buffers in otherwise overcommitted diaries.

I have recommended the use of time margins for busy in-house counsel and the feedback has been favourable. Some in-house counsel opt to create a 30-minute daily margin during the mid-afternoon to cater for meetings which run overtime, unexpected calls and overflow work. Others prefer a 2-hour margin on a weekly basis. In each case, creating margins becomes a self-discipline on how to be realistic and recognise limits. If margins are constantly being used up through new, unanticipated obligations, then there is a corresponding need to revise existing margins and consider setting new ones.

Manage email to avoid overload

The fourth skill which can help in-house counsel do high-value work is to manage email properly. Among the challenges facing in-house counsel is email overload. Although research in the United States suggests that the average email inbox in 2006 received about 87 messages per day,[11] there are in-house counsel who regularly receive more than that. In these circumstances, it is important to suggest some techniques to manage email in order to reduce the risks of email overload:[12]

- *Check email at defined times during the day, preferably limited to 20 minutes each time.* For many in-house legal counsel, two or three times per day should be sufficient. Constant checking of a Blackberry may in fact waste rather than save time.

- *Answer succinctly.* Mike Davison, CEO of internet company Newsvine, has a policy of answering emails in five sentences or less.[13] In effect, he treats email like SMS. Brief replies help train his email correspondents to be brief.

- *Train correspondents to be relevant.* One suggestion is that when superfluous emails are regularly received, a two-word reply be sent: 'Relevance please?'.

- *Send out better emails by*:
  - summarising points in the subject line;
  - making explicit action requests;
  - separating topics into separate emails; and
  - forwarding messages sparingly.

- *Send out delayed responses.* A response can be typed immediately, but filed as a draft. It can then be sent when one checks incoming emails at defined times. I have found delayed responses can be an effective way to train my correspondents on my (not their) priorities. Delayed responses also allow both parties some respite from the tyranny of immediacy.

- *Ignore it.* Some emails should simply be ignored. If one is wrong and it turns out that the email is about something important, one will hear about it again. Most likely, this will be by phone.

Summary

This chapter has attempted to shed some light on how in-house counsel can more effectively manage their workload. Both survey data and anecdotal evidence indicate that managing workload is a major, if not the most pressing, issue for many in-house counsel. If not tackled well, workload challenges can generate other negative spillovers which affect the morale, productivity and overall performance of the legal team.

In tackling the workload issue, I have suggested a three-step solution. First, it is important to have a basic understanding of what in-house counsel work is all about. This work is no longer only about black-letter law and other technical legal skills. It also encompasses elements as diverse as team building, managing external lawyers, partnering with key internal stakeholders, and maintaining high levels of personal performance.

This leads to the question as to how in-house counsel can accurately determine what is high-value work for them in their organisational context. The process of sifting high-value work from lower-value work will help generate the expectations which in-house counsel will be evaluated against. That process will also assist in-house counsel to decide when to say 'yes' and when to say 'no' to requests for help.

The final step revolves around how the high-value work can be performed well. To that end, several useful skills and habits are discussed. Many, but not all, have a time management aspect. They range from the habit of using the important/urgent matrix to distinguish important from merely urgent tasks, to tips on how to manage email in order to avoid email overload.

Obviously, the above three-step process of managing workload is not a panacea for all workload challenges confronted by in-house counsel. Organisational contexts, industry sectors and individual preferences differ and these differences may affect how in-house counsel workload can be managed in a specific environment. However, in many cases this three-step process will help address at least some of these workload challenges.

---

1   Team Factors, *ACLA/CLANZ Legal Department Benchmarking Report 2008*, Wellington, 2008, p 9. The other key pressing issues are: 'attracting/retaining/motivating good lawyers, and demonstrating the value of the legal department' (p 55).

2   Ibid, p 41.

3   Ibid, p 41.

4   Peter Drucker, *The Effective Executive*, Pan Books, London, 1970, pp 24–5.

5   Stephen Covey and A Roger Merrill, *First Things First*, Simon & Schuster, New York, 1994, Chs 1–3.

6   This has led to some management strategists coining the term 'attention economy': Thomas H Davenport and John C Beck, *The Attention Economy: Understanding the New Currency of Business*, Harvard Business School Press, Cambridge, 2001.

7   Readers familiar with Stephen Covey's classic work, *The 7 Habits of Highly Effective People*, Free Press, New York, 2004 (first published in 1990), will recognise some of his ideas referred to in this section.

8   Covey, 2004.

9   For a quick way to learn about one's circadian rhythms, see <http://www.bbc.co.uk> then 'Science & Nature', 'Human Body & Mind', 'Sleep' and 'What's Your Daily Rhythm?'.

10   Richard Swenson, *Margin: Restoring Emotional, Physical, Financial and Time Reserves to Overloaded Lives*, Navpress, Colorado Springs, 1995.

11   For research on email overload, see Danyel Fisher et al, 'Revisiting Whittaker & Sidner's "Email Overload" Ten Years Later', Microsoft Research, 2006, available at <http://www.research.microsoft.com> then search for 'email overload'.

12   These tips are drawn and adapted from Steve Robbins, 'Tips for Mastering E-mail Overload', 25 Oct 2004, originally released by Harvard Business School Working Knowledge. Now available at <http://www.steverobbins.com> then 'Articles', 'Overcoming Email Overload'.

13   See Mike Davison's blog: <http://www.mikeindustries.com> then 'Blog', and search for 'five sentences'.

4

PROFESSIONAL DEVELOPMENT FOR IN-HOUSE COUNSEL: WHAT'S NEXT?

by

Jil Toovey

Jil Toovey is Director of IKD. Established in 1999 as a wholly-owned learning and development subsidiary of Freehills, Melbourne-based IKD became an independent niche consultancy in mid-2008. Jil has worked in the area of business education and leadership development for over 25 years, including designing and delivering professional development programs for some of Australia's largest in-house legal teams. Jil's qualifications include a Bachelor of Arts and a Diploma of Education from Monash University and a Graduate Diploma of Training and Development from the University of Melbourne.

Introduction

The in-house counsel role is evolving as organisations respond to changing pressures. These pressures include the expansion of the global market, technological developments, increasing regulatory requirements and the ongoing demand from business for their lawyers to think commercially. These and other developments are affecting the skills, knowledge and attributes which in-house counsel must develop as valued professionals.

In addition, lawyers are typically ambitious individuals who strive to progress their careers rather than sit comfortably in the same role year in, year out. Obtaining a law degree is the first step in a professional journey that will inevitably require ongoing learning and education. Quality professional development is an imperative if there is to be career progression and capability enhancement.

This chapter explores specific issues relating to the professional development of in-house counsel. Development typically results from an appropriate balance of work experience and professional education. As the in-house counsel role evolves and matures, professional development offerings must also adapt to these changes.

At IKD our focus is on the development of in-house counsel's non-technical skills and abilities. This is because ongoing technical skills development (for example, updates on changes in black-letter law and improved drafting skills) for in-house counsel is relatively easy to obtain. For example, black-letter law CLE sessions conducted by law firms are in abundance. For the purpose of this chapter, professional development for lawyers is focused on non-technical skills — typically involving leadership, management and other soft skills — which enable in-house counsel to provide an invaluable service as business enablers, thought leaders and people leaders in their organisations.

What is professional development?

From the outset, it is important to have a clear idea of what constitutes 'professional development'. Terms like 'learning organisations' and 'executive education' have become popular and the notion of education in the business setting is seen as a lever for change. In fact, given the pace and intensity of business competition, executive education is increasingly viewed as having a role in driving an organisation's change efforts.[1] In-house legal teams are responding to this trend by dedicating their off-sites to programs that upskill lawyers in areas that will help them support and drive business strategy.

Professional development, executive education or individual learning in an organisational rather than academic context should be designed to enhance overall professional effectiveness. At its best, professional development is one of the key drivers that enable lawyers to distinguish themselves in their profession. Development should attend to two key areas: a person's current effectiveness in the role; and the development of his or her potential. Ideally our career pathways are focused on longer-term ambitions and goals so that decisions about what is and is not learnt are meaningful.

Professional development for lawyers can be provided both formally and informally. On-the-job learning and incidental learning are both vital. But they can vary in effectiveness; witness the experiences of articled clerks whose on-the-job learning can differ significantly. Similarly, formal programs that are customised to specific role needs can be highly effective or useless depending on the intelligence and sophistication of the program design and the learner's attitude towards learning.

IKD's research and the professional development needs of in-house lawyers

With that understanding of professional development, it is next important to ask the question as to whether in-house counsel appreciate the need for non-technical soft skills in their roles. If the answer is yes, then professional development of in-house counsel in respect of soft skills is important. If the answer is no, then the issue becomes less relevant.

In order to answer this question, IKD undertook qualitative research over a number of years. In 2000, IKD initiated an investigation into the role of in-house counsel in Australia. In 2005, IKD conducted a follow-up survey intended to extend and build upon the findings of that initial research. A total of 53 in-house counsel representing the manufacturing, finance, health, telecommunications, state government and professional services sectors participated in the 2005 research. Participants ranged from junior counsel with several years experience to general counsel with more than three decades of post-admission legal experience. The goal was to undertake an in-depth qualitative survey of Australian in-house legal counsel as to how they perceive their role.

The 2005 survey questions included the following:

- What do you enjoy most about your role?
- Which elements of your role would you happily give away?
- What professional development would assist you to be more effective in your role?
- What professional development would assist you to perform at an outstanding level in your role?
- Is there a legal professional you consider to be your role model?

- What does the senior executive team expect you and/or your team to contribute to the business?
- What development (industry, economic, environmental, technological, social and/or political) has had the greatest impact on in-house legal professionals in the last five years?
- What do you see as the greatest challenge for the role over the next three years?
- What has been the greatest learning for you in the role of business lawyer?

The 2005 survey report addressed the multi-faceted role of legal counsel, the changing nature of the role, and consequential development needs of people engaged in that role.[2] Overall, the survey found that the role of in-house legal counsel remained challenging and enjoyable. However, changes in the business context mean that the demands placed on legal counsel have evolved.

The survey revealed that many of the responsibilities of and expectations imposed upon legal counsel required skills which were not acquired when individuals completed a traditional law degree. In particular, there was an expectation of lawyers being effective in people management, demonstrating 'commerciality' in the legal role, and having an understanding of how the legal function contributes to the overall risk management function of a business.

The specific areas where respondents identified areas of *current* difficulty or concern included people management, administrative and clerical tasks, budgetary processes and costing. Developing the skills to ensure in-house counsel were not treated as either commercial scapegoats or quasi-commercial decision makers also emerged as key challenges. Managing the business when there were unrealistic turnaround expectations was another common issue. Also, an enormous workload incompatible with work/life balance was a major source of complaint.

The specific areas where respondents identified areas of *future* difficulty or concern included maintaining an appropriate work/life balance, finding opportunities for career development and promotion, retaining young and talented lawyers and finding challenging work. Performing their roles within an environment characterised by increasingly restrictive regulations was also raised as an issue that would only increase in the future.

A summary of the responses from the survey is provided in the table below.

Table 4.1: IKD 2005 survey summary[3]

Questions to in-house legal counsel   % response*

What do you enjoy most about your role?	
Being part of the business	85%
Variety and diversity of the role	85%
Which parts of your role would you happily give away?	
Administrative tasks	68%
People management	55%
What would help you to perform outstandingly?	
Better people management skills	79%
Developing stronger leadership skills	62%
What does your executive team expect from you?	
Contributions to risk management	75%
Help in making commercial decisions	51%
What recent development has had the most impact on your role?	
Technological developments	66%
Increased regulations	53%
What is the greatest challenge for in-house counsel?	
Maintaining a work/life balance	32%
Keeping in pace with legislative changes	32%

* Responses do not total 100% since the survey participants can provide more than one response for each question.

Of particular interest were the responses to the question: 'What would help you to perform outstandingly?'. The most frequent response (79%) revolved around 'better people management skills'. In other words, respondees were stating that non-technical soft skills were important if they were to perform outstandingly in their organisations. Accordingly, if the results of the survey are taken to reflect the views of Australian in-house counsel generally, then it is clear that the professional development of in-house counsel has to take into account the development of these needed soft skills.

Soft skills and raising the effectiveness of the in-house counsel role

The results of the survey — in particular, the recognition that better people management skills are much sought after by in-house counsel — have been corroborated through anecdotal comments arising from IKD's work in designing and delivering professional development programs for in-house counsel.

The comments arise in the following context.[4] At the basic level, in-house counsel are expected to know the law that is relevant to their business and industry, understand the business strategy and operations, and provide useful and accurate advice in a timely manner. Business executives also ask for advice written or communicated in a comprehensive and no-nonsense way.

If in-house lawyers are keen to go beyond the basic requirements, they can move beyond the 'what' and explore the 'how' by focusing on their value-add to the business. At this discretionary level they learn to navigate around the business and build relationships with key players. They understand the internal functions and form interdependent relationships with them. They deepen their understanding of the key drivers of different areas within the business so that they can act as an effective intermediary between law firms and regulators.

At this point, the importance of legal knowledge may begin to shift to second place. The in-house-counsel's business and industry knowledge, coupled with effective interpersonal skills, become critical. As in-house counsel strengthen this skill set they become better equipped to influence the business.

Once this skill set is mastered, the ambitious and highly effective in-house counsel will begin to step back and reflect on the value they can add at a more strategic level. By doing so, they move to the highest level and generate distinctive performance. They begin to ask themselves: where is the business going and how can my knowledge, skill set and experience assist us to get there? How can I take on a proactive rather than reactive role? When do I need to be a specialist and when do I need to be a generalist within the business? How can I use my intellectual and analytical abilities to assist the business to outperform its competitors?

What is significant is that through input from in-house counsel who participated in IKD's programs, it became clear that non-technical soft skills are essential for the higher levels of performance. More specifically, to be distinctive in their roles, individual lawyers and legal teams must develop the non-technical skills relating to leadership; influencing; managing team performance; innovation; managing organisational politics; relationship management; and commerciality.

In reality, however, the traditional law school education and initial training for lawyers do not cater well for the development of such soft skills. Law students learn advanced thinking skills when it comes to critical analysis and objective and detached reasoning. Then, for most law graduates, the law firm environment in either commercial or criminal law is their introduction to working in their profession.

For some, the transition from private practice into the role of an in-house counsel within a business or government department is an obvious and often attractive option. The transition experience is commonly a story of relief as lawyers contemplate a working life without timesheets. They feel excited about being closer to the 'real action'. If there is a personal interest in the product or service the organisation produces then the prospect of practising as an in-house lawyer is even more attractive on both a professional and personal level.

With the shift to an in-house role, a new realisation emerges. In order to contribute significant value to a business, an in-house lawyer must develop knowledge about the industry, regulators, internal strategy, products and services, operations and the personalities and drivers of key internal stakeholders. In contrast, progression in private practice results from greater specialisation or a deepening of expertise in one area of the law.

For the lawyer transitioning into or growing within an in-house counsel role, a view of self based largely on technical expertise can become an unconscious but significant hurdle. This is because the in-house role is typically a more generalist role compared to a lawyer in private practice. However, if an individual's identity and credibility are based on being an expert, then the transition to a generalist role can be a significant challenge.

Although deep technical knowledge may be a relevant focus for some in-house counsel roles, often a high-level understanding of the law combined with an understanding of how the law will either drive a business outcome or prevent a disaster can be a greater contribution. Also, to be effective, in-house counsel must translate legislation to meaningful business information. Business people are uncompromising in their request for all legal advice to be provided practically and in the context of their business issue. In this instance the in-house counsel assumes the roles of translator and influencer, because they are required to influence the business to make a decision that will protect or advance business or organisational interests in the longer term.

The challenge for those who make the transition to an in-house role is to feel comfortable with an awareness of the legislation and an understanding of when work needs to be briefed out to an external specialist, because the outcome will protect or advance the business from a commercial and strategic perspective. Moreover, if the career objective is to move towards the role of general counsel, then professional development must focus on strategic thinking, networking and influencing.

Effective general counsel are those who are able to strongly influence business decisions at executive and board levels while building a high performing legal function that is seen to be a vital part of the business by internal clients. They also manage the organisation's relationships with law firms well. I have found that to perform at a distinctive level, they tend to rely less on their technical skills as opposed to their leadership, management and soft skills. These skills are even more important if the general counsel wishes to transition away from a legal role into a business role — in which case the art of thinking commercially and the skills of relationship building must be the focus of professional development.

Lawyers learning soft skills

If soft skills are important for the in-house counsel role, how can they be learnt? One of the more insightful ideas which can inform this discussion is that of the 'reflective practitioner', as elaborated by the respected MIT educator and theorist, Donald Schön.

A key message from Schön's research into the difference between a good professional and a great professional is that good professionals are likely to 'reflect on action'.[5] They do this by looking back on an experience and considering what it is they might have done differently to achieve a better outcome. Great professionals, on the other hand, develop a skill which enables them to identity the moment when they need to change their approach to get a great outcome.

This moment is significant because it is the point in time where the individual can choose to continue along the path they are on, or stop and reflect on alternative paths. The act of identifying 'the moment' and taking one's full intelligence to optional responses is a level of mastery that develops with experience. Inherent in Schön's concept of 'reflection *in* action' is the notion of not knowing. We stop and reflect because in that moment we become aware that the intended course of action or response may not work.

Schön's concept of reflection in action raises a particular challenge for lawyers. This is because the concepts of not knowing, ignorance and risk taking can be counter-intuitive for those who undergo a traditional law school and professional legal training. While the admission, 'I don't know' is perhaps the most progressive and confident statement an individual can make because it opens up possibilities of new knowledge and learning, for many lawyers, 'I don't know' can be a statement that evokes deep anxiety because their credibility relies on their role as a technical expert.

This is not to devalue the technical expertise which lawyers have. Neither is it deriding the risk-averse nature of the legal role, which is both legitimate and necessary. In the context of providing legal advice the conservative approach is understandable given that the consequences of making errors can be extreme. Litigation, reputation and financial costs are the potential results of incorrect or indefensible legal advice in a business setting.

However, when risk-averse behaviours limit learning and development it becomes a problem. From my experience working closely with lawyers, it appears that the fear of failure and intense criticism of self and others are common traits among lawyers. The focus on the negative aspects of everything can, over time, develop a pessimistic frame of mind (one which many lawyers seem not to consider strange or problematic). Interestingly, psychologist Martin Seligman has this comment regarding lawyers and their training:[6]

> Lawyers are trained to be aggressive, judgmental, intellectual, analytical and emotionally detached. This produces predictable emotional consequences: he or she will be depressed, anxious and angry a lot of the time.

More specifically, through my experience of working with lawyers, it often seems that expressing anxiety or insecurity is seen by many lawyers to be seen a sign of weakness. Providing and receiving positive feedback can be counter-intuitive after years of mental training that is focused on the identification of flaws. Intellectually, this strong metal training and agility can be demanding and stimulating. Emotionally, however, this mental framework can be draining, demoralising and isolating. In the extreme, it can produce individuals who are at the top of their game but feel they are underachievers.

The common unconscious questions which I have come across among lawyers relating to perfection ('When is it good enough?') and expertise ('Who is the expert in the room?') can minimise the enjoyment that can come from professional achievement. Coupled with the constant drive towards high achievement, winning the case or closing the deal, this creates an enormous pressure to succeed. Not surprisingly, in some jurisdictions, lawyers are now understood to be one of the professional groups most likely to experience depression: 'When adjusted for socio-demographics, lawyers topped the list, suffering from depression at a rate 3.6 times higher than employed persons generally'.[7]

For these reasons, professional development programs for lawyers must provide the emotional safety that ensures that lawyers feel comfortable to take risks and experiment with new information and skill development. Strong coaching skills which help them to absorb positive feedback and self-assess objectively will heighten the integration of learning and counter their overdeveloped ability to self-criticise. A good understanding of these issues provides an opportunity for those in positions of influence to drive heightened self-awareness and development opportunities for lawyers that build resilience, self-confidence and a deeper enjoyment of the role. A broader acknowledgement of the impact which legal training can have on self-esteem, ego and satisfaction for lawyers as professionals is an imperative for professional development to be effective. Without due respect for the unconscious issues lawyers deal with, professional development programs for groups of lawyers can only have limited success.

How lawyers best learn

Traditionally, lawyers were trained in the master–apprentice model. In our current context, this model translates into learning on-the-job. Even now there is a level of comfort with this model because knowledge and experience are being passed from one generation to the next and hierarchy is respected. From this, it would be incorrect to assume that all lawyers have the same learning style; nevertheless, it is possible to speculate about the kinds of learning experiences that lawyers generally find attractive.

In the first instance, the presenter must have credibility and experience. The content to be presented must be solid. In addition, any theory must be relevant to actual challenges in-house counsel face in their roles. The workload is generally intense and in-house counsel are often time-poor. From that perspective any investment in learning must be seen as adding significant value to their day-to-day interactions and tasks.

Inviting critique, providing forums for debate and enabling insight through reflection and discussion with peers are approaches that are likely to be effective to upskill and develop lawyers. An intellectual challenge with opportunities to apply or practise a new method or approach is unlikely to fail once credibility is established.

Ways to build the in-house legal team's capability

What specific professional development methods are there to help build and expand the capability of in-house counsel and their legal teams? Essentially, the primary options include coaching and mentoring, internal development programs and external development programs. The decision as to who should be undertaking what type of professional development is typically in the hands of the general counsel, the learning and development function of the organisation or, in a large in-house legal team, there can be a role dedicated to this task of lawyer's professional development. Below I consider the benefits and risks of each of these options.

Coaching and mentoring

As mentioned earlier, the traditional way to train a lawyer has strong alignment with the master–apprentice model. This model acknowledges the hierarchy at the heart of the profession. It is also well aligned to the professional because it minimises the risk of a young lawyer applying legal principles inaccurately. Finally, it is likely to engage the learner given the disdain lawyers can have for those outside of their profession and the respect they have for those of their own, especially those with experience.

For this reason, in many legal teams mentoring is a key professional development tool; the advantages are obvious. The disadvantages are less obvious to anyone who has little expertise in education. Formal or informal coaching and mentoring requires an understanding of the coaching and mentoring role as well as knowledge about different techniques that will result in an effective transfer of learning.

Generally, I have found that lawyers are very good at asking difficult questions. However, their education trains them to ask a question with the answer in mind. In my experience, such a position is not conducive to effective coaching or mentoring. Moreover, for professions like law and medicine there are specific challenges when it comes to on-the-job learning. The risk of mistakes and failure is significant and the time available for quality coaching and mentoring by more experienced professionals is limited. From an organisational perspective, salaries are high and there is a need to secure a return on investment. These dynamics present a challenge for both disciplines when it comes to professional development through mentoring and coaching.

Internal learning programs

Many of the larger government and corporate organisations offer professional development programs that focus on leadership, relationship and influencing skills. The value of these programs for lawyers includes the basic skill development in addition to the relationship building and networking with individuals and groups within their own organisation. However, the downside is that the generic nature of these internal programs also means that it is unlikely that the educational designer or facilitator has a deep understanding of how the legal mindset best learns.

External learning programs

External professional developments programs designed specifically for lawyers are valuable if they have been consciously designed and are delivered with the lawyers' specific learning needs in mind. The time spent addressing the deep cynicism of many lawyers — which can be an ultimate blocker to learning — is time well spent. There are also key benefits for in-house lawyers networking with their peers from other organisational settings.

Trends impacting the in-house legal role

In the final part of this chapter, I wish to discuss some of the key trends impacting the in-house counsel role (which are also impacting business) and how these trends can affect the future professional development of in-house counsel.

Increasing levels of activity by regulatory bodies, a global business environment which has given rise to fiercer competition, technological advances and concerns about broad social responsibility and ethics are all issues that are challenging business leaders. Executives are under increasing pressure to perform and manage multiple and often conflicting forces. If in-house counsel are to demonstrate their value, they need to maintain a balanced focus on their own domain while tracking developments in the broader business environment.

Demonstrating the skills required to team up with the organisation to deliver great outcomes is a key requirement for lawyers who want to succeed in the current and future environment. While this challenge may sound intoxicating for lawyers who want to experience the cut and thrust of business, it presents a number of fundamental issues for lawyers given their professional obligations. The effective in-house counsel will have to know when they need to operate in the role of risk manager and when they need to take up the role of business enabler. The need for this transition will only intensify in the future. To be effective and appreciated, in-house counsel will need to become more adept at modifying or even switching roles. The external business and regulatory environment itself is shifting at an ever-increasing pace.

In addition, we are now seeing new generations entering the workforce with unprecedented expectations about their career options and an ambivalent attitude towards senior members of their workplace community. While the experience and knowledge of older practitioners are still valued, to the savvy Generation X and Y lawyers who live in a global community, their elders can seem primitive and underdeveloped, especially when it comes to technology. Generations X and Y are feisty about their rights and they expect to have time with their seniors for the purpose of mentoring.

Another assumption that may be shifting is the common understanding between the in-house counsel and the organisation underpinning the investment into professional development. The cost is high in terms of both time and financial resources no matter how such professional development is delivered. The return on investment in the past was loyalty. With the dynamics of the global talent market and the changed relationship young professionals have with the work, loyalty can no longer be assumed. That said, effective professional development initiatives can be a way for organisations to demonstrate commitment to staff and retain motivated and talented in-house counsel.

Summary

This chapter has provided a snapshot of how important soft skills are for in-house counsel who wish to function effectively in the increasingly complex and regulated business environment. The professional development of in-house counsel in respect of these soft skills thus becomes a critical issue. At its best, properly undertaken, such professional development can dramatically improve the value and contribution of in-house counsel to their organisations. However, there are some mindset hurdles which must be overcome before such professional development programs can succeed. Overcoming these hurdles will increase the value which the legal function contributes to the business and enable lawyers to develop and grow in their in-house roles.

---

1   See generally, Jay Conger et al, 'Executive Education in the 21st Century', *Journal of Management Education*, 1 February 2000.

2   IKD, *The Role of Legal Counsel — Survey Conducted by the Institute of Knowledge Development,* unpublished report, Melbourne, 2005.

3   IKD, *The Role of Legal Counsel – Survey Conducted by the Institute of Knowledge Development,* June 2005.

4   The following description of required performance, discretionary performance and distinctive performance has emerged through my discussions and practical work with in-house legal teams. It is possible that these concepts are rooted in some conceptual models initially developed by a management theorist; however, to date I have not been able to find a specific published reference to that effect.

5   Donald A Schön, *The Reflective Practitioner: How Professionals Think in Action,* Basic Books, New York, 1983.

6   Martin Seligman, *Authentic happiness: using the new positive psychology to realize your potential for lasting fulfillment,* Random House, Australia, 2004, p 181.

7   Seligman, 2004, p 177.

PART 3

*L*eading the Legal Team

5

STRATEGIC LEADERSHIP FOR THE IN-HOUSE LEGAL TEAM

by

Will Irving

Will Irving is the Group General Counsel of Telstra, Australia's largest telecommunications company. In that role, he leads a legal team of more than 100 lawyers who provide legal solutions and strategic advice to Telstra's board and business units. A graduate of the University of Melbourne with degrees in commerce and law, Will was previously a lawyer with Mallesons Stephen Jaques. In 2006 ACLA named him the Australian Corporate Lawyer of the Year. Will has also been recognised globally as winner of the 2008 International Bar Association's Communications Law Committee Award for outstanding achievement by in-house counsel.

Introduction

Most general counsel find it very difficult to give priority to the longer term and to make the time to focus on strategic leadership. We find it relatively easy to think about the commercial and legal issues at hand in a tactical way. That is what we have been trained to do and, typically, have had years of practice doing. Likewise, managing a steady state business is also relatively straightforward in comparison to transforming a business or an in-house legal team.

What often seems far harder is to turn the telescope away from looking in the direction we are heading at present, and instead focus on how to change the outlook for our businesses, ourselves and our legal teams.

However, thanks to the explosion of regulation in every developed economy, as today's general counsel we are in a unique position to use our knowledge of business, law and the world around us to step beyond the more traditional role of a reactive lawyer waiting for our clients to call. We can now actively suggest legal strategies to a business to meet its challenges in ways which it may not otherwise have considered.

The increased strategic role enjoyed by general counsel parallels that experienced by CFOs — these days, the de-facto deputy CEO in many companies. The control and use of information by today's CFO makes their role far more important than the less valued and more technical role of Director of Finance some 20 years ago.

Likewise, the general counsel, working together with the director of human resources, is very well placed to help shape the evolution of an organisation's culture, beliefs and behaviours to assist its long-term legal and ethical health. Together, we assist our organisation not only to improve its performance in the short term but, by influencing behaviours and culture, in the long term we assist its very survival. Indeed, in recent years, it has been the failures of ethics and concomitant frauds that are the most common reasons for major company collapses or near-death experiences.

Characteristics of strategic leadership

This leads me to what I think of as the four key characteristics of a legal team which has effective strategic leadership. By this I mean not only that the legal team is led strategically by the general counsel, but that it contributes to the strategic leadership of the organisation. In my view, such teams typically:

1. have an outward looking attitude;
2. know the importance of a 'change is an opportunity' and 'let's try this' culture;
3. have excellent legal skills and are ethically strong, commercially astute and, hence, highly respected; and
4. actively try to shape the internal (and possibly the external) environment in which the team operates.

Some may think that these four characteristics are in the wrong order. However, without the first characteristic, the ideas that drive the second will be hard to spot, and developing the third will also be very difficult. While a legal team may generate many ideas internally, there is much that can be learned from the successes and failures of others inside and outside the organisation; this makes having an outward looking attitude essential. It is only then that the remaining three characteristics become real possibilities. From there you will be in a position to provide leadership more broadly.

There is a fifth element not mentioned above that may be relevant depending on your organisation and its unique circumstances. That is the shaping of the external legal and regulatory environment. While this is a critical component of work for general counsel in heavily regulated industries (and the telecommunications sector in which I operate is certainly one of those), it is less relevant to most in-house counsel most of the time. Thus, this chapter will focus, and elaborate, on the four that are most relevant to all in-house counsel.

An outward looking attitude

Having an outward looking attitude is common to many in-house counsel; it is part of what has taken us from behind the desk at a law firm and closer to the coalface of commercial life. Unless we are interested in what our organisations do; what they are thinking about doing; what threats they face; and what opportunities may arise or (most importantly) be created, we cannot hope to be good in-house lawyers.

Knowing this, it should not be too much of a stretch to read widely and remain engaged with what other in-house lawyers are doing via corporate lawyers groups like ACLA in Australia; ACC in the United States; CLANZ in New Zealand; and your local law society. For bigger legal teams, the trends in the larger, more legally constrained economies such as the United States and Europe can be tracked via groups such as the General Counsel Roundtable.

Having an understanding of business theory and staying up-to-date with what the great minds in the leading business schools are thinking and writing can also be very useful. At a personal level I find a subscription to the *Economist* and the *Harvard Business Review* for global issues and local legal publications such as *Australasian Legal Business*, *ACLA Journal*, and *Lawyers Weekly* for domestic issues, is worthwhile. These are great publications for skimming while travelling or during the daily commute — for those of us lucky enough to have accessible public transport.

A 'change is an opportunity' and 'let's try this' culture

This is possibly the hardest thing for many lawyers. As those in the Telstra legal team know, we have tried a lot of things over the years; some have worked brilliantly while others have had a well-deserved quick demise.

As a leader, while you have to think carefully before making decisions, above all you have to make decisions. If you want to engender a culture where change is not seen as threatening, you also need to be prepared to try and to fail and not lay blame. The lessons you learn the hard way are the lessons learned best (though hopefully by watching others you can reduce the severity of your mistakes and the frequency with which they occur). I am often reminded of a cartoon I was given as a university student that summed up this idea. It was Garfield the Cat saying: 'If people are supposed to learn from their mistakes, I should be a genius by now'.

By definition, changing embedded attitudes means doing things that have not been done before and taking your team (and probably yourself) out of your comfort zone. So, although there is the risk of making your own mistakes, at least if you are getting out there and making them you have a chance of being on the path to success. Not doing anything means entropy is eating away at your current capabilities.

Granted, there are times when it is wise to wait for more information on which to base a decision or to proceed slowly, especially where the hearts and minds of others will take time to follow. However, if you aspire to lead well then you need to have a bias for action. You have to get over what for many lawyers is a prime motivator of their success and attention to detail — a fear of failure. To quote a senior manager who left Telstra many years ago, a North American: 'You can't shoot the moose if you're sitting in the lodge'.

Of course, 'shoot, ready, aim' is not a smart way to operate either. But, in my experience, lawyers have a tendency to wait too long before making decisions. They do not trust enough in the possibility of fixing things 'mid-flight' or in taking calculated risks before you have every detail tied down. When we look at the commercial managers we work with, we often find that those who are most successful have the ability to go ahead with imperfect information and are flexible enough to change course to a smaller or greater extent if circumstances subsequently dictate doing so.

Implementing a 'let's try this' approach will, however, depend on whether the broader culture of your organisation will permit this. This means that, at the organisational level, the 'way we do things round here' is a critical element in any legal team's understanding of itself, its ethos and whether new initiatives will succeed or fail.

Building and maintaining a legally excellent, ethically strong, commercially astute and highly respected legal team

Building and maintaining a world-class legal team is not an easy thing. In simple terms, it requires getting the best raw material you can in terms of the legal and personal qualities of the lawyers you hire. Then, it is applying the world's best practice tools, systems and professional development, together with a cultural overlay, to turn them into the best lawyers they can be and at the same time have them regenerate and perpetuate the team and its culture.

Shaping the internal (and possibly the external) environment in which the team operates

George Bernard Shaw once said (decades before gender neutrality became a reality): 'The reasonable man expects to adapt himself to the environment, the unreasonable man expects the environment to adapt to him, therefore all progress depends on unreasonable men'.

That, however, does not mean that the reasonable person has no place in the legal team. It does mean that you should not be satisfied with second-best (although sometimes you have no choice in the short term). If all reasonable approaches fail, it may be time to push a few boundaries and make yourself unpopular. As one of the most experienced and successful senior managers I've worked for once put it: 'I'm running the company for shareholders, I'm not running for office'. So, whether it is in terms of resourcing needs, the level of involvement of the legal team in management forums or other factors that are limiting the team's ability to deliver a world-class service, standing up for the team is critical. Of course, how you do this is very important. It takes finesse to judge the boundary line and how hard to push things before your efforts become counter-productive. While this is a higher risk strategy, if you aspire to lead strategically that means sticking your neck out from time to time. As I was reminded recently, even heavily-armoured turtles only ever move forward by sticking their necks out!

There is a significant long-term effect if we fail to shape our environment to make it a more positive place for lawyers to work in. By this I do not mean creating what is necessarily a 'cushy' environment; in fact, it often means quite the opposite. Given the kind of tight labour market that is likely to endure for some time, key legal team members will eventually leave. If you have been successful in building a very strong succession pipeline then this may be a necessary and even positive thing. If not, then by the time enough key legal staff have left and senior management sit up and take notice of your concerns, it will quite possibly be too late to recover quickly.

The hard part is to give warnings to the powers that be early and often enough that those warnings are credible, and at the same time, avoiding sounding like a broken record or getting a reputation for complaining. Each organisation is different, so there is no right or wrong answer on how to do this. A graduated message delivered one level above the level where the approval is actually required may be necessary. This is not easy. For example, unilaterally raising an issue with the CEO of your company, when it is the CFO who makes the operating decision, is not something I recommend you do without having explained the situation to the CFO first. It is easier when the message is directed at a lower level within management (as long as you have the multi-level relationships required and you do so in a way that is supportive of the management layer below).

Locking in the boundaries and judging where potential allies are located is a key skill that is outside the scope of this chapter. However, just as you would think about an external negotiation and the interests (not just positions) of your counter-parties and stakeholders, so too this is very necessary when tackling difficult issues internally.

Decision-making frameworks

After the preceding discussion on the characteristics of a legal team which has effective strategic leadership, I wish to touch on the issue of decision-making frameworks. This is because leadership is ultimately judged by the speed and quality of decision-making and the way those decisions are communicated. In other words, the core building block of being able to lead strategically is having a set of internal principles to guide decision-making. Each leader will have their own set of these. Below I have set out a selection of 21 decision-making guidelines, that I have gradually refined over the years, which I consider important in a strategic leadership context. These guidelines give me a frame of reference when it is necessary to make quick decisions (hopefully these are decisions that I will not regret later or which will confuse my team due to their being inconsistent). In addition, they also enable what I hope is a consistent culture to develop within the teams that I have been privileged enough to lead.

This list continues to evolve and has a number of exceptions, nuances and hierarchies that could take an entire book to explain. However, I have tried to keep things simple by listing the most important points so as to give a glimpse of the kinds of thinking that drive the strategic choices which I think a general counsel needs to make. Other general counsel may have different views. The key is to think about your own decision-making guidelines — which may be very different to mine — and to continue refining them as your experience grows and the environment changes. In the list below, I have grouped guidelines for ease of reference, but some cut across multiple categories.

It is all about you

1. *Enjoy leading and want to lead*

   In my view, leaders are made and not born. But there exists one important caveat — you have to want to be a leader. You need to want it because you think, a little egotistically probably, that you can do at least as good a job, if not better, than those who might also be under consideration for the leadership role. You do not have to think that no-one can do it better on day one, but you do need to think that you will reach that point over time. Once you have reached that point, it will be time to start thinking about how you can bring the next generation through to do an even better job than you have done. Unless you think this way, there is a risk that you will view your direct reports as threats rather than as individuals to be nurtured.

2. *Leadership is not static*

The great leaders I have worked for, alongside or seen from further afield, consciously or subconsciously, continually evolve and learn from what works or does not work. They also recognise that leadership is dynamic. My current CEO (having led major companies on three continents) is a master at this. Indeed, whether it is business, politics, the law or elsewhere, it is the failure of leaders to go on listening, adapting, changing style and substance, which ultimately leads to their downfall. In many senses, success breeds complacency and, by doing so, sows the seeds of future failure.

3. *Strategic leadership at a personal level means working to make yourself redundant*

Yes, you read that correctly! When I was first told this by a partner at my old law firm more than a decade ago, I was quite taken aback. He had just announced that he was leaving to take up a role as a general counsel at a major company. This seemed to fly in the face of all the hard work which we more junior lawyers were doing — the whole aim of which, I thought, was to make ourselves indispensable to our clients and, by extension, indispensable to our law firm. All this was in the hope of one day making partner (most of us who came out of university during the recession of the early 1990s had a very different view of job security compared to the generation of lawyers who have followed and for whom a serious recession is hard to imagine).

Yet, the partner's logic was impeccable. For so long as you are indispensable, you are trapped; you will be letting your clients and colleagues down by leaving and they cannot afford to let you leave. Hence, they offer you more and more inducements to stay in a role from which the spark, interest and joy of getting to work to meet some new challenge have long since gone. However, if you have someone who you have groomed — ideally to the point where you feel they can now do the job better than you — then you are free. Free to delegate, free to then have the time for the more innovative and longer-range thinking that is necessary for strategic leadership. You are, ultimately, free to leave to pursue whatever new opportunities you create, or which happen to come your way.

Interestingly, that was not the last time that former partner built up a team and then, when the right time and opportunity presented itself, moved on. He is now the CEO of a billion dollar business.

4. *Leading people requires understanding that people watch their leaders first; listen second; obey third; believe in what they are being told fourth; and then only after that point will they start to advocate the same approach themselves*

While this ought to be obvious, it continues to amaze me how many leaders (whether in a business or other organisation) do not 'walk the talk'. For example, although there are times when there are good reasons for 'some staff to be more equal than others', in an area like law, the difference between the general counsel and the most recently-hired lawyer should quite often be no more than that of experience. If you are not behaving in a way that you would expect your team to behave, then before too long they will be copying what you do, not what you say. Even more significantly, if you are not treating your staff as closely as possible to the way you yourself would like to be treated, they quite probably — especially in the current tight legal job market — will not be your staff for a lot longer.

5. *Be yourself, but learn to vary your range of communication and decision-making styles*

Successful CEOs and general counsel have to be able to change styles to suit the audience. Again, you have to be yourself, but winning hearts and minds is critical and that means tailoring the delivery — not the substance — of the message to suit the audience. Every leader is an individual. Some are introverted, some extroverted, some more comfortable managing up, and some at managing down. If you are not yourself, people will see through you very quickly; you have to operate within the boundaries you are comfortable with. However, if you can, you should gradually change the boundaries within which you operate by testing out new approaches and becoming more versatile. Behavioural bandwidth matters.

Being strategic about developing your own leadership style also means working out how you get comfortable making tough decisions if you have a more collegiate style. Or, if you are naturally more directive, how do you nurture people and build consensus when this is needed? Being able to adapt your leadership style to suit the circumstances is a rare and very valuable skill.

6. *Making others look good is usually the best way to make yourself look good*

The tension between helping our immediate clients to look good in front of their superiors (or even helping the CEO present well to the board) versus the need to sometimes claim the credit is a very fine balancing act and largely dependent on the personalities involved. An advertisement that ran in Australia for Deloittes in recent years sums up what I think is the better approach. The tag line read: 'We're out for glory — just not our own'.

If the environment you work in does not publicly acknowledge the value you bring, you need a lot of inner self-worth. You also need to take some parental-type satisfaction in seeing a business do well if you are going to prosper as an in-house lawyer. If the business people do not at least privately acknowledge the value of the legal work within a company, then that can be a lot harder too.

However, if feedback is important when dealing with clients, it is even more important when dealing with your team, including support staff. The nature, frequency and extent of the feedback, recognition and reward that individuals prefer varies markedly. As those in my team know from our various attempts to improve how we do this, there is a wide range of preferences in a team. What some like, others strongly dislike. Versatility is very important here too.

7. *Asking questions is almost always better than making accusations or assumptions*

By this, I do not mean that you should artificially 'play dumb'. Still, it continues to surprise me how much you learn and how much better relationships are when, by way of a question, seemingly stupid behaviour is challenged, or advice that is contrary to what was hoped for by the client is delivered. Put simply, a question opens the mind of the recipient and lets that person reach the desired conclusions in a way that then makes the advice or admonition much more effective and less confrontational. This requires a high level of emotional intelligence and can be very hard to do at times.

Likewise, offering an apology for something that is contentious — even if the apology is for the form of communication rather than the substance — will often help disarm the relevant individual and allow that person to get past the personal 'face' involved. That person may, in fact, end up agreeing with you that they could have handled things differently or that your advice or proposal is the right one.

8. *If, to borrow a topic I once debated at university, 'The art of being a great lover is knowing when to leave', then the art of being a great in-house lawyer is knowing when to argue out a point internally and when to let it go*

There are times when I can imagine circumstances dictate that you really have to go to the point of resigning over a major matter of legal principle or the non-acceptance of advice you are giving. However, for almost all of the time, that is not the issue. Too often we are at the other end of the spectrum. We are holding on to our views for too long when, in fact, the legal dimension has been weighed in the mix, the business has made a decision and it is time to move on.

One way of knowing when to let go is to put yourself in the shoes of the business, and then put yourself in the shoes of an impartial observer hearing the 'case' on whatever is the issue. See how strong the two sides are. Usually this is a good way of deciding whether you really do or do not have a case to pursue.

9. *Learn to live with ambiguity, contradictions and risk*

Dealing with ambiguity and not expecting the world to resolve itself with nice, neat, binary answers are also very important. Based on the Myers–Briggs Type Indicator framework, many lawyers have strong 'T' (thinking) and 'J' (judging) scores. This suggests that such lawyers like logical, clear and defined solutions. Think Mr Spock in *Star Trek*.

Yet, in reality, the more senior you are in an organisation the more often you find that potentially contradictory or uncertain states of affairs exist. Understanding that this happens and not always wanting or needing a final resolution straightaway, and then being prepared to focus on what matters most, are often signs of an ability to think strategically and beyond the tactical and the literal.

At the same time, I am not suggesting that your core principles as a person, or the performance of your professional duties, should be negotiable. There are times when ambiguity is not acceptable and you need to take a stand. It is judging the situation you are in and how then to respond with a long term, principled, but also practical perspective that separates a strategic response from an instinctive one.

10. *There is no substitute for hard work*

As golfer Arnold Palmer once put it, 'The more I practice, the luckier I get'. In order to have both the time and knowledge to provide strategic leadership, you have to be close to your team; the business and its leaders; the legal developments that affect them; and, of course, the organisation's major legal matters. You also need to have the confidence to rely on your own judgment. That only comes with a lot of practice.

My current CEO has a superhuman reputation for hard work (think 120-plus hours a week) and 35-years' industry experience on top of that. This shows every day in the level of insight in his questioning, decision-making and strategic focus, and has led to a step change improvement in the company's competitive position.

The role of the legal team

11. *Most of the time, legal work in corporations is just a means to an end*

In private legal practice, the law is the reason for the law firm's existence. Being in-house is different. Unless you are in a business such as insurance (where the output is essentially a legal document), the legal team is not part of the core business. It is a support function. As such, if the team is not needed on an issue then that is a good thing.

Yes, the legal team can be a value creation area, not just a cost centre. But the value creation always leverages whatever it is that an organisation does to serve its customers and other stakeholders, and deliver returns to shareholders. Of course, there are times when a legal team is front and centre and certainly performs a crucial role as a protector of assets and a transaction facilitator. But, the team does not generate sales nor produce a company's goods or services. The team also needs to be careful not to stifle commercial risk-taking or longstanding relationships that help create a company's success.

At one of our Telstra legal conferences our COO made the comment that, after more than 30 years of business life in various parts of the world, what he thought set the great in-house lawyers he had worked with apart from the rest was the fact that they thought like business people in terms of problem analysis and then applied very strong legal skills to propose solutions. In contrast, the merely good in-house lawyers thought like lawyers (that is, in technical legal terms) for whom the business was just a very important client.

In reality, being a great in-house lawyer means seeing the law as a source of competitive advantage and a means of both solving problems and creating commercial opportunities. Few non-lawyers, in my view, stop to consider that large areas of business are built purely on legal products. Insurance is the most obvious area, although some complex mathematics has been added to determine how to measure the legal risks being allocated by contract.

For many regulated industries too, the value creation available from rigorous and innovative lawyering can be very significant. In my own industry, in the 1960s and early 1970s, the first major competitor to the incumbent AT&T in the United States was a company known as MCI. The company was once described to me as starting out as a law firm with a communications tower on the roof. Indeed, MCI's most valuable assets in its first years of existence were various regulatory filings seeking market access.

12. *Within the bounds of your ethical and professional obligations — such as your duty to the court and the importance of your independence as a legal advisor — your job is to advocate your organisation's position, whether you agree with it or not*

At times it can feel like the business people have all the power. This can be difficult in circumstances where the outside world assumes that you agree with everything your organisation does or that you advised them to take a particular course of action.

The imbalance of power — where the client calls the shots, while the lawyer is to act on their instructions — does not help. Yet, this is a fact of life.

It helps to remember that everyone is responsible to someone: staff to their superior, CEOs to boards, boards to shareholders and regulators, regulators to governments, and governments to voters. We too are responsible to a higher authority than our organisations — the courts. For, so long as client legal privilege remains potentially available to our clients for our work, we must always remember that our professional independence is a key source of our value.

Leading your team

13. *Who you recruit matters a great deal*

My comments earlier that you should work to make yourself redundant does not mean that everyone you hire has to be the next you. If your team is focussed on volume work internally, this will also apply less. Every team needs its share of valued and experienced professionals, not just aspiring general counsel. However, unless you are already recruiting a proportion of people who you think are at least as talented, and likely to be at least as good in-house lawyers as you are once they have had the experiences you have had, then you should make that your first priority after you put this book down. Moreover, that proportion should increase the more you rely on external firms for volume-based work.

In addition to your lawyers, focus too on your support staff. Not only are your support staff the face of your team to your clients, they are essential to your team's productivity. For all the effort that often goes into getting an extra 5% in productivity out of lawyers, having great support staff and the right systems and tools can add multiples of that for much less effort and expenditure. I find it helps to remember that your support staff are in a similar position in relation to the lawyers as the legal team as a whole is to the rest of the organisation — they are an essential function that can create real value if managed well.

14. *Management styles and behaviours matter*

When it comes to selecting your team leaders or direct reports (assuming your team is at a scale where not everyone can report to you) it is very important to choose a variety of personality types. Appointing a series of clones is an easy trap and a big mistake.

However, it is also important to be aware that if you select people whose management styles are too different from your own or those of your organisation, then one of two things are likely. One possibility is that the friction created will become intolerable and a 'divorce' will be very time-consuming and potentially destructive. Alternatively, you will fail to monitor those people properly and may allow behaviour that should be stopped. Immense damage can be done if this occurs over an extended period. There are times when you may not even be aware that it is happening. Hence, the monitoring or skip-level meetings that you do in these cases takes on a much higher level of importance than would otherwise be the case.

In this respect, measuring performance on both the outcomes and behaviours is a necessity in a legal team. Once you do this you must take action to redress poor behaviours, no matter how good the performance. In a predominantly metrics-driven area like sales, poor behaviour is often tolerated for longer. However, in an in-house context where, like it or not, we often set behavioural and ethical benchmarks for our organisations, the behaviours quickly take primacy.

15. *You cannot communicate too much with your own team*

At Telstra we have a large team of around 100 lawyers spread out geographically across Australia. We have weekly team meetings; a mix of video and audio across multiple venues (the joys of being a telecommunications company!). Telstra lawyers also receive a weekly email from me; a monthly newsletter written by lawyers and support staff in the team; and participate in sub-group meetings and fireside chats (one-on-one skip-level meetings between me or my deputy and lawyers and each member of our support staff). We also have a two-day conference each year; a PA forum for support staff that meets regularly; a 'Ministry of Fun' that is our social committee; and virtual groups of lawyers from different teams who get together on particular legal topic areas on a regular basis.

Of course, when communicating, listening is often more important than talking. As someone who naturally likes to talk a lot, I find it helpful to think about the purpose of the conversation: is it for information, empathy, thought patterns and how the person solves problems, or for an underlying message (or a combination)?

Your clients

16. *Your clients are people too and they are often far smarter than lawyers tend to think*

    Non-lawyers often do not (and cannot be expected to) understand the complexities of the law in many areas. In the same way, lawyers, particularly those who are relatively new to an organisation or have not spent time outside the law, can fail to understand the complexities of many commercial roles.

    In particular, in many legal teams, there are (hopefully) nice clear lines of authority. This means we know where our jobs begin and end; what our professional obligations and ethical duties are; and what we are trying to achieve — to give the best impartial legal advice we can.

    In contrast, quite often in business the objective is far less certain. What the objective should be is not always agreed upon and then the lines of responsibility can become blurred. Indeed, in my experience, one of the things that lawyers moving into non-legal roles struggle with is that they are accustomed (whether they realise it or not) to having the train tracks laid out for them in terms of their roles. However, in commercial life, the greater flexibility in many managerial roles means that the boundaries are less obvious. Where does one manager's job begin and another end when both rely on each other's teams for inputs crucial for them to be able to deliver on their KPIs?

    In my experience, legal teams that are well-organised have far fewer issues with internal politics than many business teams. In contrast, it takes very strong and experienced commercial management to bring real clarity when it comes to business roles. This complexity, combined with the multidimensional nature of many commercial roles, means that in large organisations the things that the lawyers think should be easy can be, in fact, very difficult.

17. *Some people find it very hard to publicly acknowledge the role that lawyers play, but that does not mean they do not value the lawyers' role*

Managers who understand how important their lawyers are and recognise good lawyering will, by their actions and in terms of involvement, signal that they value the work of their lawyers. Sometimes, just being in the room is a signal that you are valued. However, some lawyers too often feel the need to have more positive affirmation and find it hard to accept this reality.

In all this, the personalities, type of work, external environment and whether things are going well or not so well for the particular area or individual client, all play a part. The key thing is that you know (tell management if necessary) that they know that they have received great advice and that you are a trusted member of their team. If in doubt, let management take a bit more of the credit. But, if they seem to be taking your contributions for granted, then there are many polite and progressively less subtle ways to remind people that it has been the legal team that has really done the heavy lifting.

Organisational dynamics

18. *First-mover advantage really matters, whether in business or dealing with internal organisational requirements*

   Being first does not simply mean that you face less competition — that is usually only transitory. It means you learn the lessons first and if you act fast you can create a sustainable advantage by (in the words of ice-hockey legend Wayne Gretsky) 'skating to where the puck is going to be'.

   Internally, I have tried to have the legal team be an early participant in whatever new initiatives are being rolled out, be they cost cutting, quality improvement, training or other initiative. Being a small group of articulate guinea pigs has advantages and risks. But, if there is a genuine commitment to adapting the relevant program based on feedback, then there can be real advantages to being involved early.

   First, it gives us a chance to engage and influence whatever it is before the methodology is locked in. In particular, at times the legal team does not neatly fit into initiatives that may suit the bulk of the business. So, if you are involved early there is often more flexibility than after the cookie-cutter has been used multiple times and its shape is fixed.

Second, being involved early enables us to either get early benefits of the program or adjust promptly to the pain and move on, as the case may be. Often, when going on annual leave, the anticipation time beforehand lasts far longer than the leave itself and is, in fact, part of the experience. Equally, the knowledge that something unpleasant is lurking in the future is potentially very destructive for morale. Far better to get on with it, make the hard decisions required and move on.

Finally, being part of company-wide initiatives early means that we clearly show that we breathe the same air and share the ups and downs of the organisation. When progress gets reported we are in the 'already completed' category and, hence, we can build relationships with colleagues by sharing our experiences with groups that follow.

19. *Relationships with other support functions are critical*

By stating this, I am not just referring to that part of the finance team which set or help manage your legal team's budget. Most of the time, the teams from finance, human resources, public relations, regulatory, and others are themselves small groups with specialised professional functions. In practice, they can be great allies in managing complex issues.

Strategic planning

20. *Time and timing: both are key dimensions*

By definition, strategic issues are often longer term in nature and often need component pieces to be put in place in sequence. Turning around entrenched attitudes or long held but now outdated views takes both time and timing. Time is important because repeated focus on the issue, with gaps in between, may be needed to enable assimilation and minds to slowly open. Timing is also important because picking your moment (be it after good news, bad news or no news, or when people are very busy or less busy) may well have a bearing on the outcome.

For example, sometimes delaying a response to an email (even if you know exactly how you intend to reply) may result in the sender being in a different frame of mind by the time you do reply. This is timing used to your advantage. To borrow a phrase that was once used about a very successful manager I worked with, 'you need the patience of a serial-killer' part of the time.

Thinking through the elements of the Gant chart and what is on the critical path, and how to sequence things, is, of course, vital. While I have always thought the oft-quoted Sun Tzu adage that 'every battle is won before it is fought' is a bit trite, there is no doubt that you can very significantly alter the odds of winning by detailed and careful planning. 'Letting the other guy have it your way', as the negotiating quip has it, requires a lot of predictive chess to be played first.

21. *In making strategic decisions that require others to act in the way you want, the biggest challenge is often planning out and then co-ordinating the elements that need to come together; doing the persuading is then the easy bit*

Marshalling the tools required to initiate, execute and then entrench change takes time and planning. Then, finally combining all this in order to persuade the relevant authority to take the action you want at the time you want it taken requires even more careful planning. Thus, a strategic change does not happen by accident.

One of my favourite movies is Oliver Stone's *Wall Street* and in this context a quote from Gordon Gecko springs to mind: 'A fool and his money were lucky enough to get together in the first place'. Yes, luck might get you through occasionally but, more often, without a lot of planning you will be unlikely to succeed.

Conclusion

Strategic leadership is not about 'set and forget'. It is about early warning and preparedness for long range trends. It is about influencing change. It is about implementing cultural and behavioural change. It is about learning as much as you can from your successes and, more importantly, from your failures.

You will have noted that I have often referred to cultural and behavioural change. This is because changing operational processes — for example, if there is a faster, cheaper or better way available to do the same activity — is often not so much strategic as it is tactical.

This tactical change is more about attention to detail and follow-through.

On the other hand, successfully changing behaviour, building political capital and marshalling resources requires envisioning the future. It requires potentially making significant changes in your personal behaviour and that of others, combined with longer-term thinking, longer-term implementation and longer-term results in mind. This is what strategic leadership is about.

6

THE GOVERNMENT IN-HOUSE LEGAL ROLE: SIMILARITIES, CONTRASTS AND CHALLENGES

by

Bruce Brown[*]

Bruce Brown is Special Counsel for the Commonwealth of Australia Department of Finance and Deregulation. He previously held legal management positions in ASIC and the ACCC. In 2006 and 2007, he was the National President of ACLA. He is also a chartered company secretary (FCIS).

Introduction

In my role as president of ACLA, I often found myself talking with mixed groups of in-house lawyers from the private (or corporate) sector and the public sector. The thing that has always struck me is that in-house lawyers in both sectors have far more in common than they have which is different.

In this chapter, I will discuss the main similarities and differences which I see as characterising government in-house legal roles when compared to corporate in-house roles. I will also touch on the question of 'who is my client?'. This is a key question which continues to generate debate among in-house lawyers from both government and corporate sectors.

Similarities

From my perspective, there are several key similarities in government and corporate in-house legal roles. Some similarities are in the form of common challenges and others are common constraints imposed by the nature of legal practice.

Value of service

The key challenge which both government and corporate in-house lawyers will most commonly describe is the need to be seen by their employer as something other than a cost centre. The simple reality is that an in-house legal unit's real value is often not capable of measurement in the same way as the organisation's sales or shipping department might be. Much of the value we add is, in fact, in terms of minimising liabilities and risk management for our employers. Preventing or minimising a disaster is often incapable of being valued — particularly if no-one in the boardroom or the departmental secretary's office realises that a potential disaster was there to be successfully averted in the first place.

To have a team of professionals who are embedded in the organisation, with an intimate knowledge and understanding of its culture and activities (and the specific areas of law that relate to those activities) and who are effectively 'just down the corridor' is of enormous benefit to an organisation. Too often, however, the value of an in-house team is assessed by a simple comparison of the hourly cost of an in-house lawyer and the hourly rate offered by an external law firm.

Using external lawyers

The second most common topic is what legal work should be undertaken in-house, and what work should be farmed out to the external law firms. The factors that guide this decision in a government legal unit are essentially the same ones that drive the decision for the corporate in-house lawyer. Most in-house legal units in both sectors tend to focus on developing their expertise in the areas of law most relevant to the particular work of their employer. The two main situations where work is briefed out are where specialist legal advice in other areas is required, and where the in-house unit does not currently have the physical resources to undertake the volume of work required.

There can be an additional layer of considerations for the government in-house lawyer, in that there may be Legal Services Directions promulgated by the Attorney-General which prescribe certain restrictions on the practice of government lawyers. These tend to be in the areas of court litigation (but not tribunal work) and in relation to the settlement of claims.

The next major reason why an external lawyer may be briefed is because there are occasions in both the public and corporate sectors when the secretary of the department or the CEO needs to have a written piece of legal advice that has the signature of a partner of a major law firm or a silk attached to the last page. This may be for the benefit of the board or Cabinet, or a major third party in a commercial transaction, in order that they can be satisfied with the 'independence' of the advice. The legal advice itself may actually not even be very complex. Galling as that can be to some in-house lawyers, it is a simple fact of life that they all learn to live with. What more experienced in-house lawyers recognise, of course, is that often this is done as part of risk management at a strategic level by the organisation, and simply represents a proper transfer of risk outside the agency.

Following on from the decision as to which work should be outsourced, I find that in-house lawyers naturally move onto the common issue of how to properly manage external lawyers, and how to get the best value for money from them. Government lawyers are voracious readers of material from general counsel and chief lawyers in the corporate sector on how to best do this, and many of their strategies are capable of transferral into the government sector. As governments have become more aware in recent years of just how much money is being increasingly spent on outsourced legal work, they have demanded a more rigorous approach to the management of those providers.

Recruitment and retention

There is one other common topic that in-house lawyers in both sectors will very quickly get to when they meet. Recruitment and retention are becoming major challenges in the in-house community — both public and corporate. The market for young lawyers is extremely tight at the moment, and both groups struggle to meet the increasingly generous packages that the larger firms are offering to attract young blood. Not surprisingly, many young lawyers have an eye to working in London, Hong Kong or (increasingly) Dubai for a few years, and the preference in those countries is for products of the major commercial law firms. (There is some market for Australian government in-house trained lawyers in the United Kingdom, particularly in the local government area, but the attractions of that work are obviously not as strong as that of a magic circle firm in London). I have noticed an increasing trend for young government lawyers to shift to the larger firms simply to hone their commercial resumés in readiness for the big move overseas. The same is true in the corporate in-house legal world.

The major attraction relied upon when recruiting for in-house work has always been the opportunity to work up close and personal with the business of an organisation, rather than just being briefed to work on a small part of the exercise, and a legal part at that. Not surprisingly, as a result, many in-house lawyers end their careers in non-legal parts of a company or department.

Although legal managers in the public and corporate sectors are spending more of their time working on strategies for recruiting and retaining good lawyers than ever before, there is one button that government legal managers can push that is not as generously available to their corporate counterparts. Whereas both can extol the virtues of being able to work intimately within an organisation, and be involved in projects from start to finish, government in-house lawyers can also be rewarded with heavy exposure to policy work. It would be unusual for any government lawyer to not be involved at some stage of their career in the development of government policy.

Obviously, in part, this is due to the fact that much government policy is implemented through legislation — an area where lawyers have a natural advantage. The other main reason, I find, is that government organisations are always keenly looking for people in their ranks who can 'think well and write well'. Lawyers, because of their training and discipline, fit this description aptly and so they still tend to predominate in the policy areas of many departments.

In-house lawyers are always attracted to the possibility that they may be able to have a personal involvement in the development of a government program that may affect millions of Australian individuals or thousands of corporations directly, whether it is in the area of tax reform, housing reform or the development of a new approach to dealing with Aboriginal issues. It is not surprising, therefore, that many in-house government lawyers ultimately move out of the legal area and become attracted to policy development or program delivery areas.

There is one other advantage that government legal managers can offer young lawyers which is usually not capable of being matched as generously in the corporate world. Although private firms and corporations are offering their young lawyers increased support and opportunities to undertake postgraduate work, it is a simple fact that government departments, both state and federal, can offer greater opportunities for sponsored further education.

Many departments offer cadetships and graduate trainee programs which include financial support to undertake masters degrees. Some also offer opportunities for students to work in departments and provide financial support for their undergraduate studies. Some departments have even entered into arrangements with particular universities to offer specialised masters degrees and graduate diplomas in relevant areas of law. Ongoing support in terms of giving their lawyers time off to study is scrupulously adhered to. Although firms and corporations support these kinds of initiatives, there is no doubt that their commercial imperatives limit the amount of time and money they can apply to such young lawyers. Providing opportunities for a young lawyer to enhance their academic qualifications is one area where the government does have a major marketing advantage.

Career progression

One characteristic that the government and corporate lawyer share is that they work in an environment that, structurally, militates against them spending their entire career in the legal stream. Much is written these days about the decreasing opportunities for reaching a partnership in a law firm. For the typical government in-house lawyer, like the corporate in-house lawyer, the issue is more acute since career prospects tend to narrow fairly quickly. Granted, the government in-house sector has grown significantly in the past eight years. However, the bureaucratic structure of government has always had a dampening effect on the ratio of partner-equivalent lawyers to employed solicitor-equivalent lawyers.

In the private sector, the ratio of employed solicitors in a firm to partners may be as low as four to one. In the government sector, however, the ratios are much higher. It is not uncommon for a senior executive lawyer in a government department (roughly equivalent to a partner in status, but not in remuneration) to have between 15 and 20 employed solicitors answering to them, and many departments only have one senior executive lawyer in their structure.

The turnover of senior executive lawyers in government is also extremely low, and hence, many experienced in-house lawyers often reach a stage where they need to make decisions about where their careers are going. Some move into the private sector (into corporations that work in the same space as their former department), and some move into non-legal positions. Others give much higher priority to enjoying quality of work in their department of choice.

Admission and practising certificates

Another area of commonality between government and corporate in-house lawyers relates to admission and the take-up of practising certificates. Almost all government lawyers are admitted as legal practitioners of one of the Supreme Courts of the various states and territories. To my knowledge there is no mandatory requirement in law that a government in-house lawyer must be admitted as an officer of the Supreme Court before they can provide legal advice, but it is certainly the standard expected in almost all government agencies and departments.

The question of whether they also need to hold a practising certificate is more complex. For a long time, because of the view that most government lawyers were only serving one client and the public at large was not at risk, there was not a large take-up of practising certificates by them. This tradition was assisted by the fact that most departments would not pay for practising certificates for their in-house lawyers because they were not a compulsory requirement for working as a government lawyer.

This attitude has changed significantly in recent years, and government lawyers in many departments and agencies now hold practising certificates, just like their corporate sector counterparts. A major driver behind the change in this attitude was the increasing sophistication of the law in Australia relating to when legal professional privilege could be claimed, and the desirability of strengthening the department's case by having its advice provided by in-house lawyers who hold practising certificates.

Rules of conduct

One final area of commonality between government and corporate in-house lawyers which I wish to mention relates to their rules of conduct. Lawyers in the private sector and in-house lawyers in the corporate sector are bound by one set of rules and standards of conduct as officers of their respective Supreme Court, and a further set if they hold a practising certificate. These standards also apply to most government in-house lawyers. In addition, however, there are two sources of standards of conduct which specifically apply to the government in-house lawyer. These are the various public service standards and codes of conduct that apply to any government officer, and the Model Litigant obligations.

All state and territory governments, and the Commonwealth, require government in-house lawyers to comply with public service laws. In-house lawyers who are Commonwealth public servants, for example, 'are required ... to behave at all times in a way which upholds APS [Australian Public Service] values'.[1] Those values include obligations to:[2]

- be apolitical, performing functions in an impartial and professional manner;
- have the highest ethical standards; and
- deliver services fairly, effectively, impartially and courteously.

They are also all obliged to comply with various codes of conduct. The Australian Public Service Code of Conduct includes obligations to:[3]

- behave honestly and with integrity;
- act with due care and diligence;
- disclose, and take reasonable steps to avoid, any conflict of interest (real or apparent); and
- not make improper use of inside information.

All these statutory value statements reinforce or add to the ordinary legal profession obligations that a government in-house lawyer must comply with.

Finally, a government in-house lawyer is expected to comply with the Model Litigant Obligation — a common law based principle (see *Melbourne Steamship Limited v Moorhead* (1912) 15 CLR 133 at 342) which sees all government agencies being expected to not take advantage of their size and resources when conducting litigation against private citizens. Some state governments and the Commonwealth Government have actually taken the step of enshrining this principle in law. The Commonwealth Attorney-General, for example, has issued a set of Legal Services Directions under the Judiciary Act 1903 (Cth), which impose a range of obligations on departments and their lawyers relating to the use of legal services (both internal and external) and how legal affairs should be conducted. Those directions include extensive rules on how to act as a model litigant, and the responsibility for ensuring that these rules are complied with will often fall on the in-house lawyer.

Differences

After detailing what I see to be some of the key similarities between the government and corporate in-house roles, it is also useful to outline some differences. Although arguably not as numerous, they should be articulated and acknowledged.

Lawyer overload

Although in-house lawyers in the corporate sector will often face the same structural restrictions on opportunities for advancement in the legal stream as their government counterparts, there is one feature they will rarely if ever face in their corporate environment. That is lawyer overload. In many government departments, lawyers and law graduates are becoming a significant portion of the population. This is particularly the case in those departments which have a major policy function, or which have a major regulatory, litigation or commercial function. Lawyers are still only found in limited numbers in the more traditional program delivery agencies.

For example, when I worked in the ACCC, the agency employed 450 staff, of whom 147 were legally qualified or law graduates working towards their admission (usually through undertaking courses at the Australian National University or the College of Law). Officially, however, there were only 25 positions in the entire agency that were described as legal positions.

Conversely, the Health Insurance Commission (now known as Medicare Australia) employed 4,000 staff, of whom only 14 were lawyers. Twelve were in the legal branch, one was an in-house lawyer who had been promoted into a management position, and one was a partner of a law firm who sat on the commission's board of management on a part-time basis.

Many departments in both the state and federal areas now have very active graduate recruitment schemes which are major parts of their staff recruitment strategy. Many of these recruits come from the burgeoning number of law faculties spread around Australia (reflecting the desirability of recruiting those 'smart people who can write well'), and so it is becoming far more common to come across law graduates, if not qualified lawyers, in departments, often starting their careers by working in areas that have nothing to do with the law.

In the corporate world, this trend is far less noticeable. Except, perhaps, for some merchant banks and legal publishers, lawyers and law graduates are still commonly found only in the legal division of a company.

What does this mean for the government in-house lawyer? It is very much a double-edged sword. In many respects, the lawyer in a department that doesn't have too many lawyers has a perverse advantage in that the work of the lawyer is often still seen as having a certain mystique. In a department where lawyers are seen as being 'a dime a dozen', it is hard to maintain much mystique about what you do. Often, your client may be a former lawyer who is working in a non-legal position. The good ones will recognise that they are not there to second guess your work and they will leave the lawyering to the lawyers (unless you are so completely wrong in your advice that even they cannot help themselves). The bad ones will simply try to do your job instead of the ones they are paid for.

Ultimately, lawyers have egos. There is nothing quite as smugly satisfying for a lawyer who has been out of the game for a few years, in a management or policy position, who can show they've still got their razor sharp legal skills by quibbling with a young in-house lawyer over a point of no consequence. Thankfully, these types are rare and most clients who are lawyers will be supportive of the legal branch. A good lawyer also usually makes a very good instructing client, because they know what you need to know in order to provide them with useful legal advice.

Shadow legal branches

Another more insidious risk that arises from the large number of lawyers and law graduates in some departments, however, is that if the in-house legal team does not deliver a good service to its clients in the department, then shadow legal branches will quickly start to appear. These can take various forms. It might be a policy area that already has a large number of lawyers on staff, and which starts to self-advise on legal issues. It might be a branch that specifically sets out to recruit a lawyer for an apparent non-legal position and then uses that person for legal services. In some instances, a branch that has a number of lawyers who came to the department through its graduate recruitment scheme over a number of years will start to use them for paralegal work and, ultimately, for legal work.

By controlling what comes within the definition of 'legal work', a client branch that is not happy with the department's in-house service provider can also very quickly marginalise the in-house unit from its activities. The other alternative, of course, is that many departments permit their branches to seek legal services directly from private law firms and an in-house legal unit may find that their clients are going to external sources for their advice. The shadow legal branch is a risk that the corporate in-house lawyer does not face to the same extent as the government in-house lawyer.

Unique government organisations

There is one other characteristic of the government department that gives the provision of legal services a special flavour. It is that each department is, by definition, unique. Except where it sets up a number of agencies to manage a specific role in different regions (such as regional water management or health services management authorities), the fact is that any government tends to establish only one department or agency to undertake each task allocated to the state or Commonwealth. In Australia we do not, for example, have multiple police forces or education departments in each state, and in the Commonwealth we do not have multiple income tax agencies or departments that deal with foreign affairs.

Because each department has a unique role, it is by definition a unique blend of different applications — such as policy, regulation, project management, revenue collection, and others. There is no such thing as a standard departmental structure or culture. This has meant that the suite of legal needs of each department is unique, and the manner in which those needs are best met can vary significantly.

In 2006, the Australian National Audit Office produced a *Better Practice Guide — Legal Services Arrangements in Australian Government Agencies*.[4] This was a follow-on from its major performance audit review of legal services in the Commonwealth in 2005. One of the most significant points made by the Auditor-General in that guide is that there was absolutely no 'standard' structural model for legal services across the agencies and departments of the Commonwealth. In large part, this is because of the factors described above. A similar comment would apply to the states and territories. However, in the smaller states and territories it is common to find much of the legal services function centralised in one agency, and departments tend to not have their own in-house units or, if they do, they are relatively modest in size.

My experience has been that in-house legal units in corporations tend to be structured along much more similar lines, and a corporation can usually find at least one other company (often, a competitor) which delivers a product in the same space. Benchmarking against similar corporations is easier in the corporate sector than it is in the public sector, where by definition no two departments even do the same thing.

Who is my client?

After surveying what I see to be the key similarities and differences in government and corporate in-house legal roles, it is timely to re-visit a question which time and time again exercises the minds of in-house lawyers. No topic has caused the death of so many plantation softwood trees as the ongoing debate amongst in-house lawyers about 'who is my client?'.

Only one client?

The touchstone distinction between a lawyer in a firm and an in-house lawyer (whether corporate or government) is often said to be that the private lawyer may have many clients, whereas the in-house lawyer has only one (his employer). In my experience, this is a fallacy.

A typical in-house lawyer receives instructions from a plethora of separate clients within the department or company that employs them. One of the biggest challenges for an in-house lawyer is working out how to allocate their time to meet all these competing demands for their time. I have often met in-house lawyers who will ensure they allocate particular time to meet the needs of their CEO or board, but I have never met one who gets their legal work from only one person or area in the company. If the company or department has many branches, then the pressure to meet all their needs satisfactorily is no less than it is for the private lawyer dealing with external clients. In fact, it can be tougher, because the client is not on the end of a phone line at the other end of the city — they are invariably in the office next door or just down the corridor. The physical proximity makes it harder to keep them at bay.

It is also wrong to assume that the only competing demands these branches have is for your time. Often, these clients can also have competing demands in terms of what outcomes they desire. Legal department staff can very easily get embroiled in 'family disagreements'. Client branches will try to haul the in-house lawyer in to take their side if there is a dispute between different parts of the company or department.

In a company, the sales department may have a very strong idea about how a particular advertising program should be run, whereas the compliance department may have a very strong counter view about the trade practices breach that the advertising campaign may represent. Disputes within a company about whether a particular product may breach copyright or safety laws, or whether a services delivery contract has been breached will also often arise. In the government sector, the same kind of tensions will exist. The regulation branch may have a dispute with the enforcement branch about whether a particular company should be investigated. The commercial projects branch may believe a legislative amendment is not necessary to achieve a certain outcome in a major program delivery exercise, whereas the policy branch may believe a legislative solution is essential. And everyone has disputes with the CFO and the internal auditor. A good government in-house lawyer learns very quickly how to not take sides in these exchanges — and, more importantly, how to appear to be not taking sides.

The ultimate client

As to whether the in-house lawyer has an *ultimate* client, that is easier to answer — although it is still not without its conceptual and legal difficulties for the government lawyer. The corporate in-house lawyer has, I believe, an ultimate responsibility to the company itself, as represented by the board of that company. On a day-to-day basis, their responsibility is to the CEO.

For the government in-house lawyer, there are a couple of scenarios to consider. In a strictly constitutional sense, based upon Australia's Westminster traditions, the sole client of an in-house lawyer working for a conventional government department is the Crown (often represented by a minister or a representative of the department). The Crown is an indivisible entity and so, in theory at least, government departments should never be in conflict with each other in circumstances that would lead a government lawyer to have an ethical dilemma. The truth, of course, is that departments frequently adopt different positions on different issues. However, I am unaware of the ethics of any government lawyer ever having been challenged when they have loyally advised and acted for their department in circumstances where it was in conflict with another department.

Many government lawyers work for statutory agencies rather than departments. A statutory agency is established by legislation and has a legal personality independent of the Crown. The first duty of an in-house lawyer in these circumstances is to act for the interests of the agency, as represented by the agency's board. The board may not always share the views of the government, but it may also be accountable to the government, and the portfolio minister may be able to give the agency directions under its enabling legislation. This can lead to circumstances where a government lawyer may have obligations to both their agency and their minister, although these circumstances are rare. In an agency, typically there is a CEO who is responsible for the day-to-day running of the agency. The in-house lawyer's duty is to that person on a day-to-day basis.

Moral courage

Although the instances are very rare, there have been occasions when a government lawyer has had to 'stand their ground' on an issue, primarily when someone below the board or the secretary has desired to achieve an outcome without a proper legal basis. One of the most publicly referenced examples of this involves Andrew Metcalfe, the current Secretary of the Department of Immigration and Citizenship. Metcalfe was appointed secretary of the department shortly after the release of the *Palmer Report* into the treatment of Cornelia Rau when in detention, with the brief of implementing the Palmer recommendations.

Metcalfe is a former government in-house lawyer, and he tells one very important story about his days as an in-house lawyer. At one stage, his client, who held a very senior position in the department he worked in at the time, wanted to take a certain course of action which was not only not supported by the law, but which was probably wrong in a moral sense. Metcalfe recalls that the senior officer chose to ignore his advice and his own supervisor was not willing to take on the senior officer because of the bureaucratic ramifications of what it would mean for him.

It was a moral dilemma for Metcalfe. Eventually, when all other avenues had been closed to him, he felt he had no choice but to bring his concerns directly to the attention of the secretary of the department. Once appraised of the situation, that secretary moved very quickly to deal with the issue and the rule of law was upheld. It does take a degree of courage for a junior government in-house lawyer to do this, but this story is a useful reminder that an in-house lawyer is still bound by the standards expected of a professional and, on occasion, a degree of personal courage may be called for.

Summary

From the preceding discussion on the roles of government and corporate in-house lawyers, it is clear that, at least from my perspective and experience, they share more similarities than differences in their work and operating environments. Although the differences should not be minimised, it seems to me that their similarities shine out. It was, thus, pleasing for me, in my previous capacity as the National President of ACLA, to be able to work with and represent both government and corporate in-house lawyers at a national level to further our common interests.

---

* The views expressed in this chapter are the author's own and do not necessarily represent the views of the Commonwealth of Australia Department of Finance and Deregulation.

1 This is stipulated in the Australian Public Service Code of Conduct,
   see <http://www.apsc.gov.au/conduct>.

2 For the Australian Public Service Values,
   see <http://www.apsc.gov.au/values/index.html>.

3 For the Australian Public Service Code of Conduct,
   see <http://www.apsc.gov.au/conduct>.

4 See <http://www.anao.gov.au> then 'Publications' and 'Better Practice Guides'.

7

ONE DAY OF LEADING A GLOBAL LEGAL TEAM

by

Edith Shih

Edith Shih is Head Group General Counsel and Company Secretary of Hutchison Whampoa Limited (HWL). Based in Hong Kong, HWL operates in 56 countries and has around 250,000 employees worldwide. Core businesses include ports, property, retail, energy and telecommunications, generating annual group turnover of about US$40 billion. Edith leads an in-house legal team of more than 200 lawyers spread globally and is also a director or company secretary of various HWL subsidiaries. Trained as a musician and teacher with a stint in investment banking, Edith has undergraduate and graduate degrees in Arts and Science from the University of the Philippines as well as graduate degrees in Arts and Education from Columbia University. She is qualified to practise law in Hong Kong, England and Wales, and Victoria, Australia.

Introduction

Looking back to when I first set up the HWL legal department 14 years ago, I was a one-woman band. Initially, there was considerable resistance from subsidiary companies towards the notion of requiring legal clearance for specific actions. However, considering a group of our size, it is paramount that proper accounting and oversight of legal risks is in place. With the support of senior management, our subsidiaries and sub-groups began to see the benefit of legal input. Within a few years, at their request, I set up legal departments in all the sub-groups, with a dual reporting line to the subsidiary chief executive and to me at group head office. This was in accordance with a legal policy that was set up since day one.

The legal team today has over 200 in-house legal counsel stationed in 24 countries and over 44 offices. I cannot but be grateful for the support and resources the group has provided me over the years. I am fortunate to have a team of very dedicated and loyal legal counsel in whom I can trust. For counsel based in Hong Kong, we meet on Saturdays, with each sub-group team attending these meetings in turn. So, in addition to working on specific transactions with individual legal counsel, we do see all local counsel every few weeks on a rotation basis.

For overseas counsel, in addition to our bi-weekly telephone conference meetings, I do visit overseas offices regularly. I would say we have a close working relationship. We have, over time, become a big family, with comradeship built up over the years, and I dare say a legal practice that the team can be very proud of. It has always been my principle that every counsel should feel that they are a treasured part of the team and that every one should see a career path within the company.

Below is a snapshot of what counts as a fairly typical working day for me. My diary notes were taken on a Monday in November 2007. I hope it gives an accurate picture of what it is like to lead a global in-house legal team — albeit from an Asia-Pacific perspective, given that I am based in Hong Kong.

Morning

It is 7.50am one Monday in November 2007 and I am awakened by the alarm clock. I turn and go back to sleep. The second and third alarms go off. Eventually, at 8.10am, I roll out of bed, with the pleasant lingering after-taste of dreams that emerged in the last 20 minutes of my sleep. Those are the most treasured 20 minutes of my sleep, especially when I wake up in my own bed at home in Hong Kong! Now I am awake, fresh and energised and ready to start my day.

On my way to work, I answer incoming emails. It being a Monday morning, there are not too many incoming emails to reply to. Some came through from our telecommunications colleagues in Israel on the Sunday (which is a work day in Israel). Some came from our Australian telecommunications colleagues who started their day a few hours ahead of us in Hong Kong.

As usual for a Monday morning, at the office we start the day with our weekly senior management meeting. All department heads provide updates on the work of their respective departments over the previous and coming week. We spend 30–40 minutes keeping ourselves abreast of significant activities within the HWL group's businesses operating in 56 countries.

The internal auditor reports on findings and recommendations for stock control for our Chinese pharmaceutical company listed on AIM in London. As I am a director of the company, I take a mental note to follow up with the CEO. The group is completing an acquisition of a health and beauty chain in Russia later on that day. I advise the group treasurer of the amount required for completion and the timing for funds remittance with written payment request and instructions to follow. Co-ordination will be required in the afternoon as Moscow opens for business when remittance of funds and collection of title documents of the business acquired will be taking place.

In addition, I advise the meeting that legal documentation for our 3G operation in the United Kingdom to share its telecommunications network with T-Mobile is close to finalisation. Signing should take place during the week when board approval is obtained. The network sharing transaction is beneficial to both parties as capital expenditure and depreciation for further build-out of cell sites are much reduced and both parties will have a more efficient and much improved network.

The finance department advises that the group restructuring in the People's Republic of China to capture more favourable tax treatment on withholding tax on dividends and interest income is progressing as scheduled.

Human resources announces that the group employee headcount worldwide reached 250,000, and remind management of the group's Family Day scheduled for the coming Sunday. The Family Day is a fun day for over 10,000 employees and their family members. There are lots of games and presents — and, of course, the star attraction is the presence of the Chairman of HWL, Mr Li Ka-shing. He will officiate the opening ceremony, with employees participating in the opening march. The lucky ones get to take photographs with our chairman, who is always most accommodating.

Back to my office after the meeting, I find several colleagues requesting to speak to me. First, my senior China counsel takes me through an urgent real estate auction in China. As a substantial deposit has to be paid on winning the auction, we need to coordinate with our parent, which is also our co-investor, as to funding logistics. We also need to analyse the Hong Kong Stock Exchange listing rules implications on connected party transactions and organise requisite announcements.

Then, my corporate secretarial manager shows me a mock-up of the meeting papers for the Audit Committee meeting to be held on Friday. In accordance with listing rules requirements for good corporate governance, the meeting papers need to be dispatched at least three days before the meeting. A few sections are still outstanding. I call up our deputy CFO and request for the missing papers to be produced, reminding him that all meeting papers have to be dispatched prior to 5pm that afternoon.

I then return the telephone call of the CEO of our United States office in Seattle. She advises me that the employee incentive plan set up for United States employees has been finalised and options are ready to be granted. As the group's shareholder approval for the plan has already been obtained at the previous AGM, as soon as the appropriate remuneration committee and board have formalised their approval of the grant, the options can be granted.

It is now 10.30am; time for the Australian 3G management meeting and board meeting. This time, the meeting is held by video-conference. The team comes to Hong Kong on alternate months. We go through the presentation by the CEO; CFO; Sales and Marketing Director; CTO; and General Counsel. It looks like the Australian business has eventually taken off, and subscriber intake has been increasing steadily. The board meeting approves KPIs for the third quarter and their release to the market.

Noon

At noon, the HR Manager comes by to go through my preliminary year end bonus and salaries increase proposal for the legal and corporate secretarial departments. I am extremely fortunate to have a team of very dedicated, hard-working and loyal colleagues. They have exerted consistent efforts throughout the year and deserve to be rewarded. During difficult years when the general economic climate was not so encouraging, they have been patient with the company and stayed on, putting in more hours and taking up heavier workloads. They should not be disappointed this year.

My secretary then reminds me that my Thailand General Counsel is on the line with our external counsel on an intellectual property court matter. This relates to the brand used for our CDMA mobile phone business in Thailand. After an update from our external counsel on the hearing the previous day, we review the status of our opposition and determine the strategy going forward, to ensure that our position is protected. I am glad to note on the phone the return to the Thai team of a legal counsel who left the group for about two years. I extend a warm welcome to him and make a note to circulate a memo to the worldwide legal team regarding the return of our Thai colleague.

On the group's intellectual property work, I take pride in our team's success on Project Stealth. After the sale of our 2G network 'Orange' in the United Kingdom in early 2000, the group returned to the United Kingdom to invest in 3G telecommunications. We successfully undertook a program of brand registration worldwide for the brand '3'. We achieved this without being detected during the incubation and protection engineering period of three years; hence, the project code name.

We methodically designed and implemented an application program for registration of the trade mark '3' and about 400 variations around the world in 47 countries in up to 10 classes, using a combination of third party agents and anonymous intellectual property rights-holding vehicles. Where we had to acquire '3', we improved on our negotiation skills and paid less and less for each acquisition as we got better at strategising and haggling.

On the day of the brand launch, it was most gratifying to see the brand being successfully kept as a secret, without being sabotaged and with relatively little hiccups. This '3' brand, in my mind, is a versatile, energetic, and fascinating one. And it continues to evolve and develop as it matures. It has the same potential, if not more, as 'Orange' which the group created in the early 1990s.

Lunchtime

It is already 1:00pm! I hurriedly change into my exercise gear and go for my work-out. Unfortunately, I do not get to follow this routine every day. There are weeks when I can manage two or three exercise sessions a week, and weeks with none at all. I have to work harder at this regimen — but I really hate exercising! There are, from time to time, work-related luncheons and I could be tempted to give up the exercise session. Today, I dutifully spend 20 minutes on the treadmill, 15 minutes on *tai-ji* and finish up with 10 minutes of stretching and weights. Then I shower and head back to the office.

Back at my desk, while I have a quick lunch of fruit, salad and soup, I go through the master program for the forthcoming Group Asian Legal Conference. Over the past few years, it has become routine for group legal conferences to be held in Europe and Asia, in alternate years. Our legal conference last year was held in Vienna. About half of our legal counsel from the group's European operations and selected counsel from the rest of the world participated. This year, the conference will be in Hong Kong again, for expediency and cost-savings considerations.

After ascertaining topics of mutual interest and concern for the group as a whole, with the help of my general counsel, I will determine and invite the most appropriate speakers to speak on various topics. This could be a member of our team or an outside guest speaker. Our tailor-made conference is catered entirely for our own needs. We normally hold our conferences towards the end of the week, with delegates gathering at the venue on Thursday for a welcome dinner. We spend the entire Friday on topics of common interest which every legal counsel attends. On Saturday we have break-out sessions when we divide ourselves into smaller groups, normally by businesses, to consider issues pertaining to specific businesses.

The legal conference is not just for our counsel to learn the law or legal practice, or to share our 'house view' on specific issues. It also provides a forum for us to get to know our colleagues, to exchange views and expertise, and to build our own network amongst ourselves — be it with counsel from the same business or across countries and offices. Two of our most popular recurring topics are, 'What did we mess up?' and 'What are the key lessons learnt?'.

Due to work and budget constraints, not every legal counsel gets to attend every legal conference. We take turns in participating to ensure that there is a good mix of skill sets and fair opportunity for everyone to get involved as an attendee or a presenter. We also spend some leisure time together during the weekend. We get to know our colleagues better than just professionally and build up a bond as a team.

As we collect views from counsel around the group, the conference topic and theme begin to take shape. The organising team works on the booking of venues; organisation of activities; preparation of presentation materials; and invitation of speakers. There is growing excitement fuelling tremendous energy and enthusiasm in the air. Other than mega-size newspaper headline transactions, winning a piece of important litigation, or yet another award or recognition from legal institutions, I would consider the legal conference as one of the highlights of the activities of our legal department.

By the time I finish lunch, I have come up with another draft of the master conference program. This will be circulated to team leaders, within and outside Hong Kong, for another round of comments.

Afternoon

The visitors from the London city firm arrive. They have come to introduce their senior partner to me. I invite a range of my senior team to participate in the meeting including my deputy and the legal counsel heading our financing transactions, telecommunications procurement work and China work. After exchanging pleasantries, I introduce our respective teams and provide an overview of our businesses. In addition, I provide a general description of the areas of law in which the firm could possibly be of help to us, and our expectation as to work quality, reporting line, service level and fees.

As the visiting firm has recently worked on a transaction with the group, I also provide certain feedback as to their performance. The department keeps a report card system of external counsel. Our legal counsel record comments of relevance on firms that we have worked with; comments pertaining to their strengths and weaknesses, and observations of special interest. The assessment is shared within the group. As Head Group General Counsel, I approve the engagement of external counsel for better control of engagement of legal services.

We do not only receive law firms in our offices; we sometimes visit them also. For local firms, I gather selected counsel from various divisions and spend around an hour every year over lunch or in an informal meeting with firms that we instruct on a regular basis. This gives my colleagues a chance to share their views and requirements openly and collectively. It also provides a forum for our external counsel to become updated on our group business direction and our needs in specific practice areas.

For overseas firms, on a less hectic business trip, I set aside around an entire day to meet with our external counsel. These meetings, which might be perceived by both parties as a public relations exercise and of little actual monetary value, are in my view actually very useful for fostering better understanding between clients and firms. This results in better coordination and overall efficiency in our working relationship — a better partnership overall.

The Group Managing Director appears at my door, just dropping by to say 'Hello'. My office is the first in the suite of executive offices, so I regularly see executive visitors as they pass by on their way in and out of their own offices. The director is leaving for Europe that evening and wants an update on the status of the group's regulatory proceedings in Europe. I duly give him a rundown of the status on various fronts as well as progress made generally. He appears to be satisfied with the information provided and I take the opportunity to go through with him the proposed schedule and agenda for the Chairman's upcoming European management review to take place in a month's time. The director makes a couple of suggestions, which I gladly incorporate.

An assistant asks to interrupt the conversation. Discovering that the director is in my office, he has rushed over to provide me with the paperwork on the most recent order of 3G mobile handsets which requires the director's sign-off.

I spend the following hour returning telephone calls and attending to colleagues that have asked to speak to me during the course of the day. When I have some extended time in my office, my secretary makes arrangements for telephone calls to be returned and callers to be attended to. I spend more time with junior or new colleagues to ensure that they are given the necessary guidance in handling their work. My senior colleagues can be entrusted to look after transactions independently and I can rely on them coming to me when guidance is required.

Among my colleagues, I regard myself as a resource person — ready to be tapped as a sounding board, for a quick solution, the house-view, or for a historical perspective. I can also be just a friend with a listening ear. I believe heading a department does not entail only technical expertise and know-how (although those are pre-requisites). I think one of the most important attributes of a leader is the ability to enhance the development of team members such that they achieve professional and personal growth in their own right. The success of a leader and a department depends on the strength of the team members. A capable head cannot ensure the success of the whole team since he or she cannot do all the work alone. Responsibility as well as success have to be shared.

During the consultation hour this afternoon, the issues covered with my colleagues include: pre-emption rights for joint venture partners; unlimited indemnity for intellectual property rights infringement; super-majority rights for minority shareholders; and mortgage registration in China.

Then I spend some time going through, with my colleague, the joint venture agreement of our China detergent business and the procurement contract for our Indonesian network expansion. We go through the final report and the commercial executive summary of those transactions. I require that certain terms be renegotiated despite my colleague's representation of the low level of success. My stance is that we owe a duty to run the last mile and if we are still unsuccessful, we will then make a judgment call as to whether the risks can be managed through other means or be taken at all as they are.

After the consultation hour, it is time to clear the pile of corporate secretarial files in my in-tray. As I am also the Company Secretary of companies within the group, including a number of listed companies, I have a continuous flow of corporate secretarial files that I have to process on a daily basis.

The group has over 1,500 companies incorporated in 56 jurisdictions around the world. I review all corporate secretarial paperwork prepared by the corporate secretarial team before the files are disseminated to directors and shareholders for approval. Naturally, we have a great deal of new learning to do from time to time. When I first took up the job over 10 years ago, I did have to spend considerable time familiarising myself with the files and systems. Over time, with continuous updating of our documentation and systems, and upgrading of secretarial executives and computerisation over the past years, we have a good team and a good system of precedents that we can rely on.

Being in charge of the legal department helps in that I am familiar with all the legal transactions that are sent to the directors or shareholders for approval. Hence, I do not have to spend a great deal of time on reviewing those files. Having said that, there is still a vast amount of routine and non–routine work which I have to process, including signing off approvals as a director or company secretary. Such work cannot be taken lightly. I take note of issues relating to the files processed as well as corporate secretarial, company law and stock exchange rules updates and these are referred to the corporate secretarial team for discussion during our monthly department meetings.

Late afternoon

My watch shows 5.30pm — time for our bi-weekly conference call with our Italian telecommunications team. We have had these telephone meetings since the inception of our 3G operations. Our calls are held every other week and the team would report on matters that require Hong Kong review and clearance, as well as those that do not. The conference call gives the counsel leading the transaction a chance to present the transaction and answer any queries head office counsel might have. It is also a forum for subsidiary counsel to seek direction or request for assistance on specific issues or transactions.

There are two contracts of sizable value which I ask to be discussed separately off-line, so as to avoid keeping the entire team on the line. We also hold similar legal meetings with our United Kingdom and Nordic telecommunications operations. I do not manage to attend each telephone legal meeting but I make it a point to attend those meetings from time to time. I have senior legal counsel who chair those meetings and other team members can be brought in to participate in the meetings if and when required.

My mobile phone rings. It is time for a video-telephone interview. There is a candidate for the post of legal counsel in the

Netherlands. I refresh my memory by skimming over his *curriculum vitae* while having the candidate introduce himself. I can tell that he has done his homework; at the very least, he appears to have a certain level of knowledge of the company he is interviewing for. Sometimes, it is terribly irritating to find a candidate who does not have a clue as to the company that he or she is applying for a position with. To me, such a candidate is not serious about the interview or the position.

This candidate, on paper, is well qualified for the position he is seeking. It is most helpful to see him on the small video-phone screen. Things like body language and facial expression make a difference in our hiring decisions. I have invited a couple of my assistants to participate in the interview to raise legal and practical questions as to the candidate's views on legal and business issues. It is obviously important that the candidate has the requisite legal know-how. But, for in-house counsel, it is most important that they adopt a practical approach in the application of legal concepts in business. They must be able to think outside the box and supply practical solutions. This particular candidate raises some questions as to the operations and reporting line of the legal team and co-ordination with the business unit. He possesses depth in his thinking; he will get an offer.

Evening

By this time, it is 7.15pm and I am running late for a cocktail reception for the Law School Dean of my United States alma mater, Columbia University. The reception is from 6–8pm. Oh well, I guess I could still make a dash for it! Although I did not attend the law school — in my student life at Columbia in New York City, I was studying applied linguistics — I did have a fruitful learning experience at the university and have since stayed close to it. I subsequently left New York for London to read law because I did not want to work and live in the United States for the rest of my life; I wanted to return to work and live in Hong Kong.

During those days, there were very few United States firms practising in Hong Kong, and they also practised rather specialised United States capital markets law. With a United Kingdom qualification, I was able to qualify and practise in Hong Kong. There are now an increasing number of United States lawyers practising in Hong Kong. Through HWL, I have had the opportunity of working with several United States law firms. Over time, the lines between legal systems have become fused and boundaries between jurisdictions are much less distinct today. A good counsel is one who can apply general legal expertise and acumen, and transfer these skills across different situations, jurisdictions and legal systems. The nitty-gritty local issues can be ironed out by local specialists.

I arrive at the reception, greet the dean and meet with a rather large constituent of newcomers practising law with United States as well as non-United States firms. Hong Kong is a popular destination for young United States lawyers, especially those who are looking at the China market. I am privileged to live and work in Hong Kong at this important era; one in which China is undergoing tremendous transformation and making exponential progress.

After doing my duty as a daughter of my alma mater, I cross the harbour to Kowloon to go to the Hong Kong Cultural Centre for my weekly choir rehearsal. In the car, I call my Corporate Secretarial Manager and enquire as to the status of the Audit Committee papers; no, they are not complete as yet. Our finance colleagues are chasing the auditors — it would be a late night ahead. I remind the manager to order dinner and get the team fed while working on the meeting papers. It is very important that stomachs are taken care of. This is a pre-requisite to good work and, for that matter, good team work.

I arrive at the chorus rehearsal late, as usual. I have stopped feeling apologetic for my dilatory arrivals. With Europe in full swing at 7.30pm, I really could not leave the office so as to attend the rehearsals on time. I invariably arrive during or slightly before the half-time break. With music, I am fortunate to be a good sight reader and I usually manage to read through relatively challenging scores without too much difficulty. For difficult passages, I do my homework and get them ironed out prior to the rehearsal as I like to ensure that I know my music. After the rehearsal, the music lingers in my head, with a 'tail-wind' effect that provides a boost of energy to my tired body and mind. I leave the rehearsal hall, energised and light-hearted.

I drive back to the office to check on the status of the Audit Committee papers and the completion of the Russian acquisition.

I am told that the meeting papers are almost complete. We will do our best to dispatch the papers to the overseas directors — albeit late at night — so that they can have a head start with their preparation for the meeting. Some of our directors will even turn around the meeting papers and provide comments or raise questions overnight. It is good use of our sleeping hours in Hong Kong.

My colleague completing the Russian acquisition comes in to report that the funds have been remitted and bank confirmation of the remittance sent to the seller. While the overseas team is at the offices of the seller's lawyers waiting for the seller's bank to confirm receipt of funds, the parties take the opportunity to go through again the completion documentation so that as soon as the bank confirmation comes through, our lawyers can leave with the title documents.

End of the day

I arrive home at 11.30pm and watch the local news as well as the United States and European market performance while having my late-night dinner. Tonight, I have my favourite vegetable, Chinese broccoli, and baked salmon. Being so late, I am only able to consume half of the meal. I also take my daily portion of two sardines, which the group chairman very kindly supplies on a monthly basis. The sardines are intended to help improve my deteriorating bone density; a hereditary problem within my family. 'Be sure to eat the bones as well — very important', my chairman had said. I diligently obey, most appreciative of the care and attention he has taken in my well-being.

After dinner, it is computer email time. After using (or rather over-using) my Blackberry for the past few years, my fingers are beginning to give me problems, especially the right thumb which has been taking on a disproportionate amount of repetitive pressing. In an attempt to reduce the damage, I use the computer when I am not on the go.

Then, my dear husband calls. He works in Vietnam and Bangkok during the week and we only meet up during weekends. We exchange highlights of our day and remind one another to rest, relax and go to bed as early as possible (hopefully very soon).

Then my United Kingdom Deputy calls; I bid my husband farewell. She reports on the highlights of a tribunal hearing; it is the eighth day of a 12-day hearing. I could only attend the hearing physically for the opening and the closing sessions. So, my deputy calls every night after the hearing for a quick update on the proceedings and again before the hearing starts in London in the morning (which is our early afternoon) in order to review new developments overnight and strategy for the day. Tonight, the report was that it was an eventful expert cross-examination day. Our witness did well, better than expected.

It is time to go to bed. My bedtime readings tonight are the meeting papers for the Hong Kong Standing Committee on Company Law Reform. This comprises several inches of proposals and analysis of amendments to sections of the Companies Ordinance on company names. This is my appointment for a second term on the committee. I have agreed to continue with the appointment not only because company law is so much a part of my legal practice, but also because I feel that it is time to give back to the community and the profession — to contribute my time and knowhow to society in my own small way. Tonight, I do not manage much reading. I fall asleep very shortly after I tuck myself into bed, with the lights on and the meeting file open. But I know I will sleep well and have pleasant dreams ... the meeting papers will have to wait until tomorrow.

8

EVALUATING THE PERFORMANCE OF IN-HOUSE LEGAL TEAMS

by

Benny Tabalujan and Christopher Lloyd*

Benny Tabalujan has worked in Melbourne, Singapore and Hong Kong as a lawyer, educator and consultant. With degrees in economics and law from Monash University and a PhD from the University of Melbourne, he led the team which developed the IKD LegalScores performance index for in-house legal teams. In addition to his work with IKD, Benny is an adjunct faculty at Melbourne Law School and Melbourne Business School (MBS), University of Melbourne, where he teaches in the LLM and MBA programs.

Christopher Lloyd is Professor of Business Statistics at MBS, University of Melbourne. He is managing editor and joint theory and methods editor of the Australian and New Zealand Journal of Statistics. Prior to joining MBS, Chris held a number of senior academic positions at the Australian Graduate School of Management, the University of Hong Kong, the University of Waterloo and Imperial College, University of London. Active in consulting work, Chris is part of the IKD team which developed the metrics and algorithms used in IKD LegalScores.

Introduction

Performance measurement is one area where in-house counsel and external lawyers differ significantly. Lawyers in law firms are revenue generators. Their work — typically measured in billable hours — directly generates income to the firm. On the other hand, in-house counsel's work rarely, if ever, directly generates income for their companies or government organisations. Hence, the performance measurement systems which have been developed, continually refined and applied to lawyers and practice groups in law firms simply do not work when it comes to in-house counsel and legal teams.

Yet, the challenge of measuring or evaluating the performance of in-house legal teams will not go away. Year in and year out, many from the CEO down want to see how their in-house legal teams are performing; how much value they add compared to sourcing the same legal services externally; and how well they measure up against in-house legal teams elsewhere. They want objective, quantifiable data. They want statistics to gauge how well their in-house counsel are contributing to the strategic and operational objectives of their organisation. They want robust metrics which can help them compare this performance over time.

The aim of this chapter is to discuss the task of measuring the performance of in-house legal teams. Although the performance of individual in-house counsel will be referred to, much of the chapter focuses on the performance of in-house legal teams. The reason for this team focus is simple. Based on our research, it seems clear that the human resources profession has done an admirable job in developing metrics to measure *individual* performances across a whole range of organisational and business functions, including the in-house counsel role. However, it appears that there are fewer tools for measuring *team* performance. In particular, there is a dearth of tools for measuring the performance of in-house legal teams.

Given this backdrop, the chapter is structured into three parts. First, we discuss some of the factors which make it difficult to measure the work of in-house counsel. Second, we will briefly survey what measurement systems and metrics have been used to measure in-house legal team performance. Third, we introduce IKD LegalScores — an innovative and proprietary performance index designed specifically for in-house legal teams.

Hurdles in measuring in-house legal team performance

We begin by discussing the factors which contribute to the difficulty in measuring or evaluating the performance of in-house legal teams. Some of these factors are not unique to in-house counsel. They also arise with respect to other corporate support functions which reduce risk or maximise efficiency, but which do not directly generate revenue.

Consider, for example, functions like risk management; compliance; governance; ethics; occupational health and safety; and environmental management. They all share a common feature in that typically they are not revenue-generators. Of course, assuming they are properly undertaken, they contribute directly to dimensions such as staff well-being, operational efficiency and reputational strength of the organisation. The point, however, is that improvements in these dimensions, though real, are nevertheless difficult to quantify. Unlike dollar revenue, which is easy to track, an increase in corporate reputation or a decrease in operational risk is much more difficult to measure.

Another hurdle has its roots in the common difficulty which lawyers experience when trying to price or value what they produce. The traditional method of valuing legal services, especially among law firms, is by billable hours. However, as has been mentioned elsewhere in this book (see Chapter 11), this tends to confuse cost with value. The problem is exacerbated in the case of in-house counsel because many in-house legal teams do not record time[1] and have done away with hourly billings to internal clients. Unfortunately, aside from billable hours, not much is available to replace it. In fact, for the in-house legal team, there appears to be no obvious measure of legal value which does not give rise to serious measurement problems.

A third hurdle which stands in the way of measuring in-house legal team performance is the diversity of views as to what it is that in-house counsel actually do, or should be doing. Unlike sales teams which have clear dollar sales targets, in many organisations the objectives of the legal team are more ambiguous.

Many in-house legal teams exist largely for the reason of cost savings. For example, by hiring three in-house counsel and one administrative support, the total legal fees paid by an organisation to its external lawyers may be halved. Other organisations, especially those operating in highly regulated sectors, may view their legal teams as being justifiable not only on cost efficiency reasons but because they see them as providing extra value-add in terms of strategic risk management, business governance and product development. Then again there may be the CEO who says, as a reason for having a general counsel: 'Their main job is to keep me out of jail!'. This diversity of reasons for having in-house legal teams makes the development of performance metrics difficult.

A fourth hurdle tends to lie in the mindset of in-house counsel themselves. Based on our experience, it seems that compared to some other business professionals, like marketers and sales people, in-house counsel tend to find it more difficult to articulate, promote and, if necessary, defend their value proposition. Unlike other professionals trained in business-related disciplines, lawyers seem to find it more difficult to express their value proposition succinctly and in terms which their clients understand. Many lawyers have a tendency to value their work in terms of time spent on a task. Fewer are able to express their value proposition in terms of the business or organisational objectives of their employer.

Occasionally, this state of affairs is further exacerbated by the less than positive regard others in the organisation may have for in-house counsel. Some in-house counsel have been called 'handbrakes to happiness' by their internal commercial clients. Some have been maligned as deal-blockers. Others carry the stigma of being 'legalistic' and 'not commercially oriented'. Although this is clearly not the case for all in-house counsel, the negative connotations surrounding some legal teams make it more difficult for their lawyers to articulate their value proposition.

Despite these hurdles, the pressure to evaluate in-house counsel performance is great. This stems partly from the old adage that 'you can't manage what you can't measure'. In other words, all other things being equal, improved management requires improved metrics. This is even more pressing for large in-house legal teams which control or influence annual legal spends of tens of millions of dollars. Given the sums at stake, it is not surprising that senior management teams want to measure the performance of their legal teams in order to manage them better. On this point, the great American jurist, Oliver Wendell Holmes, appeared to have been uncannily prescient when he noted over a century ago: 'For the rational study of the law, the black letter man may be the man of the present, but the man of the future is the man of statistics and the master of economics'.[2]

What is available?

What performance metrics or statistical measures are available to help in-house legal teams measure their performance on a fairly rigorous and consistent basis? The short answer is: very few.

In asserting that there is little that is available to measure in-house legal team performance, we are not ignoring the significant strides which HR professionals have made in developing all kinds of performance yardsticks for individual staff.[3] The HR profession has a burgeoning sub-sector devoted to metrics, assessments and analytics which help organisations measure individual staff performance. The common acceptance of KRAs and KPIs — as well as a host of other performance-related acronyms — testifies to this.

Neither are we ignoring the efforts of key in-house counsel organisations in various jurisdictions which have grappled with this issue. To their credit, in Australia and New Zealand respectively, ACLA and CLANZ have initiated surveys and benchmarking studies in order to shed some light on this topic. In particular, the *CLANZ Benchmarking Report 2006* and the *ACLA/CLANZ Legal Department Benchmarking Report 2008* provide much useful information.[4]

In addition, several consultants — primarily based in North America — have attempted to highlight the need for additional research into the area of in-house counsel performance metrics. Specific reference should be made to Rees Morrison, previously from Philadelphia-based Altman Weil, a specialist management consulting firm to the legal profession. Morrison compiled and published two editions of benchmarking tools for in-house legal teams.[5] Yet, he was candid in concluding that, despite significant efforts and steps to improve the situation, 'current metrics cover only parts of the contribution of in-house lawyers, they fall short of proving optimal practices, and they raise many unanswered questions'.[6]

Our own research reveals that where there are performance metrics for in-house counsel and legal teams, few (if any) are widely accepted. Our findings appear to confirm Morrison's assessment that it is difficult to find metrics which adequately or comprehensively measure the contribution of in-house legal teams or which establish industry best practice.

Where there are established performance metrics such as those developed by the HR profession, it would appear that most of these apply to individual staff rather than teams. For example, the use of KPIs and KRAs for individual performance assessment is now widespread. However, few (if any) of these widely accepted metrics appraise the performance of teams; this is despite the increasing presence and contributions of real, virtual and self-directed teams in many organisations.[7] In particular, to our knowledge there are no widely accepted performance metrics which have been tailored specifically for in-house legal teams.

At the opposite end of the performance metric spectrum, the large-scale benchmarking exercises undertaken by CLANZ in 2006 and ACLA/CLANZ in 2008 are valuable in respect of the broad-based data which they provided. However, these exercises focus on broad survey outcomes. For example, these surveys tabulate the number of in-house counsel per $1 billion of revenue; or the median total employee cost (salary plus superannuation plus bonus) for in-house counsel with 5–10 years of experience. Although useful as industry or sectoral benchmarks, these ratios are often still too high-level to facilitate a more detailed performance evaluation of a specific in-house legal team.

For example, the fact that a company with AUD$1 billion turnover has 10.0 FTE in-house counsel means that it has a higher lawyer-to-revenue ratio than the Australian average of 8.0 FTE in-house counsel.[8] But what does this actually mean? Does it imply that the company is over-lawyered? Does it indicate whether the in-house legal team is delivering great solutions to the legal issues confronted by their internal clients? Does it say anything about the level of morale or operational efficiency of the in-house legal team? Clearly not. It measures the size of the team, not its contribution and much less its efficiency.

Between individual performance metrics and the broad survey outcomes across sectors or industries, there is a dearth of measures which can be appropriately used to gauge the performance of a specific in-house legal team *as a team*. Yet, from a management perspective, the value of a well-functioning in-house legal team is undeniable. To measure this value, a team-based set of metrics is desirable because it provides a means to measure the collective performance of a team rather than focusing on individuals or across sectors. Of course, this is not to say that individual or sectoral performance metrics are unimportant. What we are affirming is that a general counsel who wishes to improve the performance of his or her legal team *as a whole* must also focus on metrics designed to measure performance at the team level.

Although widely accepted team-based metrics for in-house legal teams are difficult to find, the need to measure the effectiveness, performance and contribution of in-house legal teams as a whole appears to be as real as ever. In Australia alone, we are aware of three instances in the past decade when the general counsel of large in-house legal teams commissioned major initiatives to measure in dollar terms the value of the contribution of their teams to their respective organisations.[9] While the dollar value of the contribution of an in-house legal team may, arguably, be just one aspect of the performance of such a team, the fact that such an exercise was undertaken at significant cost reveals a deep desire among the relevant general counsel to know precisely what contributions their teams were making towards their organisations. Anecdotal comments from other senior counsel confirm that they too wish to know, in quantifiable terms, the level of effectiveness, performance and contribution of their legal teams.

Introducing IKD LegalScores

It was in response to the above demand for performance metrics appropriate for in-house legal teams that IKD conceptualised, designed and produced LegalScores. Drawing on several years of experience of and research into the needs of in-house counsel, IKD assembled a small team comprising individuals with experience in legal practice, valuation of legal services and statistical performance measurement. IKD LegalScores took around two years to design. After a successful pilot in early 2008, it was launched in mid-2008.

Three dimensions

In simple terms, IKD LegalScores is a proprietary index comprising nine distinct metrics designed to measure the performance of an in-house legal team along three key dimensions:

- service quality;
- business impact; and
- operational efficiency.

The reason for having metrics measure three dimensions stems from the realisation that the contribution and effectiveness of in-house legal teams cannot be comprehensively measured using only one or two performance criteria. For example, assessing whether in-house counsel achieve pre-agreed individual or team KPIs may be a useful exercise. However, it may understate the value of that legal team if, in reality, the team was also generating additional value-add through providing legal solutions which are characterized by a high-level of commercial astuteness and business savvy.

For this reason, based on input and insights gained from working with senior in-house counsel, IKD LegalScores adopted a multi-dimensional perspective in measuring the performance of in-house legal teams. Further, IKD LegalScores also adopted a multi-metric approach to measuring each performance dimension. With nine distinct metrics measuring three performance dimensions, IKD LegalScores provides a more holistic and comprehensive snapshot of the performance of a legal team. The metrics can be accumulated if desired or can be reported separately to give a detailed profile of the in-house legal function.

Nine metrics

The unique and proprietary set of nine metrics provides the framework through which the three performance dimensions of service quality, business impact and operational efficiency are to be measured. Qualitative and quantitative data, including those obtained through surveys of internal clients and members of the in-house legal team, are put through this set of nine metrics to generate nine scores. These scores may be averaged to yield an overall IKD LegalScore for each of the three main dimensions or even, if desired, accumulated into a single score.

The nine metrics seek to measure the following performance characteristics of the legal team:

- The level of commerciality in providing business enabling solutions: this refers to the perceived level of commercial astuteness which characterises the solutions, advice and output of the legal team.

- Internal clients' perception of the quality of and confidence in the advice provided: this metric measures the level of quality perceived and the level of confidence placed by internal clients in respect of the work produced by the legal team.

- Accessibility and responsiveness to internal clients: this measures how internal clients view the level of accessibility they have over in-house counsel and the level of responsiveness they enjoy in respect of their queries.

- The achievement of team KPIs: this metric seeks to gauge how well the legal team has achieved its agreed KPIs. The KPIs measured include both qualitative and quantitative KPIs and can cover a range of performance areas including time targets, financial targets and feedback targets.

- The legal spend to revenue ratio: this metric calculates the amount of total legal spend as a percentage of total revenue of the organisation. Total legal spend is the sum of the internal costs of maintaining the legal team and the amount paid to external lawyers.

- The financial value-add generated: this metric seeks to measure the financial value-add generated by the legal team. Among other factors, this takes into account the amount of legal fees which would have to be paid to law firms if the legal team's work is briefed out to law firms. It includes adjustments for experience of in-house lawyers who deal with specific matters; the kinds of law firms used; and prevailing market rates.

- Performance against budget: this metric measures how well the legal team has controlled its costs and expenses as a cost centre against its planned budget. All other things being equal, a legal team which completes the financial year below or on budget achieves a higher score than a legal team which exceeds budget.

- Teamwork and morale: this metric measures the level of satisfaction which individual legal team members have in respect of their work environment, including work colleagues and processes. This is based on the assumption that the higher the morale, the greater the likelihood that the team will be operating at a higher level of efficiency.

- Tenure, corporate memory and experience: this metric acknowledges that the institutional memory which often resides in longer-serving in-house counsel can provide value-add for organisations by reducing the amount of re-work which has to be done from time to time.

From the above descriptions, it is clear that these nine metrics measure both processes and outcomes. For example, accessibility and responsiveness are process metrics. They are designed to measure how well a legal team's communication channels and processes work in providing internal clients with ready access to lawyers and responses for legal issues. Conversely, performance against budget is an outcomes metric since it measures how financially responsible the legal team has been in respect of controlling its costs and expenses against its budget. The incorporation of metrics which measure both processes and outcomes thus provides a more useful and complete picture of how well the legal team is performing.

Using IKD LegalScores

Designed to be undertaken annually, IKD LegalScores provides a general counsel or chief legal officer with:

- a tangible measurement of the legal team's performance;
- an independently generated value-identifier for the legal team;
- identified areas for improvement, including suggested remedial action; and
- performance benchmarking which is comparable longitudinally over time.

Each of the nine metrics is scored on a common scale with a higher number representing better performance. Because the scores have been put on a common scale, it is permissible to calculate average values. IKD LegalScores provides averages for each of the three dimensions (service quality, business impact and operational efficiency), as well as an overall average IKD LegalScore.

In practice, most in-house legal teams may wish to examine each of the three dimensions separately. The overall average IKD LegalScore should only be used for crude descriptive purposes and, perhaps, for monitoring over time.

IKD LegalScores presents the results of the legal team performance evaluation to the general counsel in both tabular and graphic form. An example of a summary graphic form for a fictitious in-house legal team is provided below. Each dimension is scaled to a mean of 70 which represents 'par value', with a score of below 65 as being 'below expectations'. The fictitious team depicted is performing above target in all three dimensions and is outperforming the benchmark most clearly in its internal processes

— referred to as the operational efficiency dimension comprising tenure, teamwork and morale, and budget variance.

Figure 8.1: Summary graph example

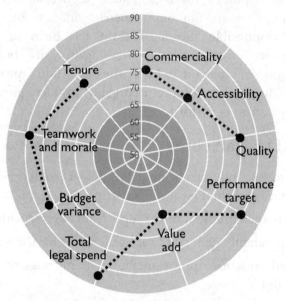

The utility of IKD LegalScores for evaluating the performance of in-house legal teams is thus obvious. It provides a relatively simple yet statistically rigorous set of metrics which measures the three key dimensions of particular interest to a general counsel:

- the service quality of the team as perceived by internal clients;

- the business impact of the team upon the organisation; and

- the team's overall operational efficiency.

Another useful feature of IKD LegalScores is its potential as a diagnostic tool. Given that the performance of a legal team is measured across three dimensions using nine distinct metrics, it is possible to use the scores as a general means of diagnosing areas of relative weakness and relative strength for the legal team. For example, if a legal team obtains a low score on the service quality dimension, it is possible to drill deeper to find out which metric(s) are lowering the service quality score. It may be, for example, due to a low score obtained for commerciality. This indicates that internal clients are rating the performance of the legal team relatively lower because of a perception that the output of their in-house counsel lack the kind of commercial realism and business orientation required by the organisation. It also follows that, in response, the general counsel receiving such a report can pursue remedial steps to lift the legal team's level of commerciality — for example, by undertaking specific professional development programs designed for this purpose.

The final point to note is that over time, as IKD LegalScores becomes more widely used by in-house legal teams, it is likely that a sizeable database of statistics will be gathered for each of the nine metrics. As data accumulates, the full database will become a rich source of information for intra-sector comparisons of in-house legal teams. In other words, the performance of legal team A operating in the manufacturing sector can be compared with that of legal team B operating in the same sector. Inter-sector comparisons can also be made. This will mean that the legal teams which use IKD LegalScores may find it easier in the future to undertake external benchmarking of their performance.

Summary

We have described the inherent difficulties of measuring the value that in-house legal teams generate. These difficulties largely derive from the diversity, and sometimes ambiguity, of legal team roles within organisations. As a consequence, there are few tools and metrics currently available for general counsel to measure the performance of their team.

The lack of easily collected and understood measures has several negative consequences. It makes the value of the in-house legal team opaque to internal clients as well as senior management. This is a serious deficiency, bearing in mind the size of the total legal spend in some organisations and industry sectors. Consequently, there is a critical need for the provision of such measures.

In response to this need, IKD LegalScores has been developed as a multi-dimensional performance measurement system, which includes metrics that measure the effectiveness of the services that in-house teams provide to internal clients; the internal dynamics of the team; and also more objective financial metrics.

The value of a rigorous objective set of performance metrics is:

- to help general counsel more clearly articulate the value proposition of their legal teams and the multi-dimensional roles that they fill within the organisation;

- to understand the performance profile of their team and, in particular, identify areas of apparent over- or under-performance;

- to monitor performance over time and to evaluate the effectiveness of initiatives designed to generate improvements; and

- as further data is accumulated, to benchmark the team against industry and sector standards.

---

*   Given the proprietary nature of IKD LegalScores, we wish to acknowledge and thank IKD for the permission granted to outline in this chapter the key features and metrics which make up the IKD LegalScores performance index. For purposes of transparency, we also wish to declare that as we are both associated with IKD, we have benefited and are likely to continue to benefit from the use of IKD LegalScores by IKD's in-house legal team clients. The views expressed in this chapter are our own and do not necessarily represent the views of IKD and any other organisation or institution which either of us is associated with.

1   A recent survey of Australian and New Zealand in-house legal teams states that the use of time recording 'was below 20% in both Australia and New Zealand; and higher in the public sector (27%) than the private sector (14%)': *ACLA/CLANZ Legal Department Benchmarking Report 2008*, p 9.

2   Oliver Wendell Holmes, Jr, 'The Path of the Law' (1897) 10 *Harvard Law Review* 457 at 469.

3   For example, see J Shields, *Managing Employee Performance and Reward: Concepts, Practices, Strategies*, Cambridge University Press, Cambridge, 2007.

4   Both the *CLANZ Benchmarking Report 2006* and the *ACLA/CLANZ Legal Department Benchmarking Report 2008* were compiled by Team Factors Ltd of Wellington, New Zealand: <http://www.teamfactors.com>.

5   R W Morrison, *Law Department Benchmarks: Myths, Metrics and Management*, 2nd ed, Glasser LegalWorks, Little Falls, New Jersey, 2001. For another consultant who has written on this topic, see R Stock, 'Key Performance Indicators for the Law Department', (March 2005) *Lexpert* 87.

6   Morrison, op cit, p 405.

7   For example, see the article: 'Taking a Closer Look at Measuring Team Effectiveness', author unknown, available from <http://www.hr.com> then 'communities', 'articles'. The article states: 'The importance of teams to the ultimate success of organisations is unquestioned. Despite this critical role, relatively few organisations have consistent processes in place to continuously evaluate the effectiveness of their teams'.

8   *ACLA/CLANZ Legal Department Benchmarking Report 2008*, p 70.

9   The person who was commissioned to undertake all three assignments, Ryszard Bliszczyk (then of Gengroup consultancy) subsequently became a consultant to IKD for the initial design work which led to the creation of IKD LegalScores.

PART 4

*R*esponding to Internal and External Environments

9

COMMERCIALITY: PARTNERING WITH INTERNAL CLIENTS

by

Debby King-Rowley and Kirsten Dale

Debby King-Rowley is principal of Burlington Consulting and specialises in leadership development, coaching, and instructional design for corporate clients across the United States, Europe, Asia and Australia. Through her consulting work with IKD, Debby has a particular interest in researching, designing and delivering programs on commerciality for lawyers and other technical experts. Debby previously held positions as Director of Executive Education at Motorola and General Manager of the Telstra Leadership Centre. Debby has a PhD in educational research from Florida State University.

Kirsten Dale is a consultant to IKD. Drawing on her work experience in Asia, Europe and Australia, Kirsten specialises in cross-cultural training, international business skills, international management training and HR consultancy. In her role with IKD, Kirsten helped to undertake, analyse and synthesise the research on commerciality for lawyers, which formed the basis for IKD's CQ (Commerciality Intelligence) program. Kirsten holds a Bachelor of Arts from Flinders University and a Master of International Business from the University of Melbourne.

Introduction

New phrases creep into the business literature, take hold, take on a meaning of their own, and then become so widely accepted that they become shorthand for communicating. Such is the phrase 'the C-suite'.

If we were to look back only a decade ago, we would be hard pressed to find references to the C-suite — perhaps because the C-suite did not exist in many organisations. There would have been CEOs and COOs, and then the list would taper off. Two people hardly comprise a suite. However, as recognition of other key leaders in corporations has increased, the title of 'Chief Officer' has been promulgated to the heads of finance (CFO), information systems (CIO), human resources (CHRO), and yes, even legal (CLO). With so many 'chiefs' around, it takes a suite to house them all. Hence, the C-suite.

For companies making the decision to recognise the suite, the question is: 'Who gets a seat at the table?'. This question is answered differently by different companies. Some organisations will have a chief marketing officer, while others will not. You will find chief technology officers in some companies but not in others. The composition of the C-suite is thus signalling two things: the core competencies of the company; and who is seen to influence top-level decisions.

The question as to who gets a seat at the table does not stop with the C-suite. Rather, it cascades down throughout the organisation. The answer at lower levels again signals what and who is considered critical to the relevant business unit. As at the company level, within the business units, the answer is largely positional. That is, a policy decision has been made that the role should be present and represented for particular issues and decisions.

However, at the business unit level, the answer also becomes heavily influenced by which person is in the role. Now consider the role of an in-house legal counsel. When is the in-house counsel invited to the table for discussions, input and decisions? In part, that will depend on the policies governing the business unit. It will also depend on how valued the lawyer is as an individual by their business partners. How will the lawyer as a person contribute to the discussion?

In particular, the level of contribution recognised by the business partners is often dependent upon the lawyer's perceived level of commerciality. In other words, commerciality (which refers to the lawyer's ability to partner with their business counterparts to achieve sustainable profitability for the business) becomes a key deciding factor in the viability of the in-house counsel.

Yet, we often see in-house counsel who do not seem to be in step with the running of the business. They live and work on the fringes of the company's core business processes. Strategic conversations and decisions are made without their involvement. They are invited into the conversation well after the key discussion has ended and the key decisions made. These lawyers' roles are seen largely as to 'review and approve' decisions that have been made by their business colleagues. As one in-house counsel commented in an IKD professional development program: 'Our business partners see lawyers as the handbrake to happiness'.

Mental models

What underlies the apparent disconnect between business partners and those in-house counsel who are viewed as not being sufficiently commercial in approach? In our view, the root problem is that they are operating from two different mental schemas. They have two different mental frameworks guiding them.

David Ausubel, a cognitive psychologist who studied learning theory, highlighted the power people's mental schema have over the ways in which they hear, interpret and remember (or do not remember) pieces of information.[1] A person's mental schema is built up over time based on their experiences and previous learning. Each person involuntarily creates their own mental schema for all sorts of categories of information. For example, we all have developed a schema for the process of checking-in at the airport. This will have been shaped by our own personal experiences of checking-in, stories told to us by others, etc. Over time, we develop a general idea of what airport checking-in means and what it will involve.

Once our schema for a certain topic is established, it works for us in a number of different ways. One advantage of having a schema is that it guides our behaviours and responses so that we do not have to focus on every detail, but can manoeuvre through situations somewhat on autopilot. For example, when we check-in for an international flight, our schema will automatically prompt us to hand over our passport at the check-in counter. This is done largely without thinking, allowing our minds to focus on other more significant things. Our schema also acts as an organiser for new information coming into our brains, enabling us to store associated facts and information together for easier retrieval and use. Our schema thus helps to organise our memory. Three other functions played by our schema are to filter, fill in the blanks and reinterpret new information.

While at times useful, these schema functions can also be detrimental in some situations. For example, Debby's mental schema for checking-in at airports has been created over a history of thirty-plus years of flying. After decades of becoming accustomed to the check-in process, and queries about preference for aisle or window seats, flammable items in her baggage etc, she was recently asked this question at the check-in counter: 'How much do you weigh?'. Not recognising the question, she asked for it to be repeated. After hearing it a second time, she responded, 'Hopefully not more than an hour, since I have a meeting I'm trying to get to'.

Debby's mental schema had filtered the question and reinterpreted it from 'How much do you weigh?' to 'How much time can you wait?'. It was only after four or five exchanges with the airline representative that she finally understood the question was, in fact, about her body weight. It seemed the aircraft she was to be travelling in was quite small (a six-seater) and balancing the weight of passengers was essential for a safe take-off and landing.

Here is a second example of our mental schema at work — read the following excerpt:

The paomnehal pweor of the human mind

It deosn't mttaer in what oredr the ltteers in a word are, the olny iprmoatnt thing is that the frist and lsat ltteer be in the rghit pclae. The rset can be a taotl mses and you can still raed it wouthit a porbelm. This is bcuseae the human mind deos not raed ervey lteter by istlef, but the word as a wlohe.

The ability of the mind to read this is based on the mental schema we have developed over years of reading experience. The beauty of schema is that we can easily make sense of things. The danger of schema is that the human mind automatically and powerfully filters information to make it fit with our individual schema or mindset. It is not that we do not want to hear what others are saying, but that our brains are working hard to help us make sense of what we are hearing or seeing. Our brains do that by reinterpreting input to align it with what we have heard and learnt previously. As humans, we tend to make sense of information within clusters and context.

We then tend to interpret within context and assign meaning to our interpretation. We then tend to act on our interpretation.

Let us now go back to the common complaint by business managers: that their in-house counsel lack commercial savvy. Our hypothesis is that this arises because business managers and in-house counsel are working from two different schema, each interpreting the same information through different filters. If this is correct, what then is the outcome?

Tribal clashes

In her book, *Tribal Warfare*,[2] Peg Neuhauser, a communications specialist, describes the specialised functions and departments that make up an organisation as 'tribes' and she postulates on the outcomes which tend to emerge when different tribes communicate. She states (at p 5):

> Anthropologically, these groups in organisations act like real tribes; they have their own dialects, values, histories, ways of thinking, and rules for appropriate behaviour. What if we took some Apaches, Cherokees, and Pygmies, added a few Japanese and Germans — plus a Texan or two — and then said to this group, 'Now go work together and get the job done!'. No one would be surprised if tribal warfare broke out in this group. And yet in many ways, this is exactly what happens in most organisations today. We create an organisation or business, we pull people together from a wide range of specialities and backgrounds, put them in a building, and expect them to work together and get the job done.

The anthropologist, Edward Hall, tells us that each tribe or culture has its own rules that govern its thinking or behaviour, and that these rules usually operate at a subconscious level.[3] We know that this is based on their different mental schema. Neuhauser describes two primary tribes: the generalists and the specialists. Generalists are depicted as those who have a broad knowledge base but who typically do not have a particular area of expertise associated with their roles. People in this tribe are often in roles such as general managers, business development, and customer relations. Specialists, on the other hand, are so named because they are thoroughly and deeply trained in a specific area of expertise, and use their specialist knowledge inside the organisation. Neuhauser illustrates the two different tribes as in Figure 9.1.

Figure 9.1

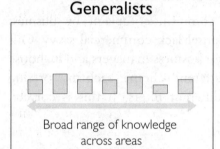

Generalists

Broad range of knowledge
across areas

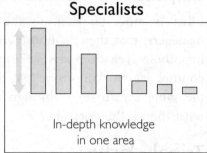

Specialists

In-depth knowledge
in one area

Generalist's Key Roles
Decision making
Persuading
Information gathering
Selling
Linking people and ideas

Specialist's Key Roles
Analysing
Advising
Researching
Teaching

In-house counsel are typically specialists. Their business partners are typically generalists or other specialists who have their own mental schema, language, values and behaviours. With this as the backdrop, we hear business partners saying, 'We need our lawyers to be more commercial'. But what do they actually mean by this statement?

In fact, our interpretation of the statement may depend heavily on our mental schema. This became very clear to IKD when we were consulting to the general counsel of a large resources company. We had been working with him and his in-house team over a period of months, and spending time within their offices. His goal was for his lawyers to be working with their business partners from the onset of any new business development, asking 'why' questions about how the proposed venture would fit within the company's overall strategic direction. He wanted his lawyers to examine the associated risks involved in the proposed venture, to look at its potential upside and downside and brainstorming options — all from a legal perspective. For example, a question he expects his lawyers to ask is, 'How does undertaking this project in China impact our potential risk exposure?'.

His legal team, frustrated with his continual behest to be commercial, kept replying they *were* being commercial. They pointed out that they were completing the advices requested of them by their business partners on a timely basis so as to not impact the closing of the deal. They pointed out that the payment clauses they inserted into the documentation worked well with the company's payments system.

In reality, there was a disconnect between what the general counsel and his lawyers were talking about. The general counsel was referring to what we refer to as 'strategic commerciality'. In his company's case, this meant a higher level of commercial thinking which focused, among other things, on China's sovereign risk and potential corruption issues. Instead, his legal team understood commerciality to mean 'operational commerciality', referring to a more basic level of commerciality which focuses on things such as the timeliness of completing legal documentation, and whether specific clauses in an agreement conformed to the company's business processes. This example highlights that our mental schema can well affect the way we do or do not understand what other in-house counsel or business partners say and do.

IKD commerciality research

Using the concept of mental schema, IKD initiated research to further understand the concept of commerciality, and to determine what can be done to help develop the commercial mindset of lawyers and in-house counsel. IKD intensified its research with an extensive research project in 2006–07 designed to investigate the relationships between business partners and in-house counsel. In particular, IKD conducted a research workshop aimed at exploring:

- the specific expertise both groups contribute within a commercial context;
- the language and dialect of both groups;
- the underlying values that drive each group; and
- the differences in thinking patterns between lawyer-specialists and business-generalists.

The research workshop was conducted using a total of 19 participants from nine organisations. The participants were split into two sample groups; one of lawyers and one of business people. Each participant expressed an interest in exploring and uncovering the different strengths and ways of thinking that each profession contributed.

The hypothesis underpinning the workshop was that specialists and generalists, based on their different mental schema, work in perceptibly different ways and that this difference may be an obstacle to good commercial relationships. These obstacles develop from preferences among business people and lawyers to assume different roles (based on different schema) when exploring business opportunities and making business decisions. For example, there may be differences in schema relating to:

- exploring risk versus minimising risk;
- focusing on concepts versus focusing on processes and details;
- being entrepreneurial versus being precedent bound; and
- generating revenue versus reducing cost.

This hypothesis was established based on academic research and on IKD's observations and experiences working with business people and lawyers over the past seven years. The methodology used to test the hypothesis comprised three exercises conducted during the research workshop. These exercises included:

- *Business case study*: The group was divided into sub-groups of lawyers and business people, with each group being placed in separate rooms and given the same task of exploring a fictional proposal for the start-up of a new business. The discussions emanating from each group were observed by IKD researchers and external performance coaches, in addition to being filmed. Behavioural, cognitive and language patterns were noted and recorded for each group.

- *Fishbowl exercise*: Lawyers and business people remained within their professional groups and participated in a 'fishbowl' exercise to discuss and observe common assumptions about what each professional group had to offer the other, and what strengths and challenges each contributed. This exercise was facilitated, observed and recorded by IKD researchers.

- *Self-disclosure*: The research participants were provided with a brief questionnaire asking them to comment, in their view, on what was required to get the best from their professional roles. The results were recorded by IKD researchers.

The results of the research workshop as reported in the *Building Commerciality Research Report 2007*[4] supported the findings of IKD's previous studies on the behaviour of specialists and generalists. During the past seven years, this work has included interactive research workshops and forums for over 300 lawyers, from both in-house and private practice roles. IKD had also investigated best practices with regard to the behaviours and skills of senior in-house lawyers, and conducted over 50 one-to-one interviews with in-house counsel. The 2007 findings suggest that specialists and generalists work in perceptibly different ways in a number of areas, discussed below.

Language and dialect

In their commercial context, business people communicated thoughts and ideas by persuading and selling, while lawyers researched, analysed and advised. Both groups used jargon and their jargon was specific to the group. Samples of jargon taken from the transcripts of business people included 'revenue model', 'market segments', and 'return on capital outlay'. Lawyers were noted to use 'dependencies', 'contingencies', 'intellectual property' and 'qualitative risks'.

For business people, their most commonly used sentence structure was the active voice. They frequently personalised their speech with the phrases, 'I think' and 'I feel'. They readily built on each other's ideas and used an iterative approach in their decision making.

For lawyers, their most popular type of dialogue was fully formed, but qualified, opinions. Their most commonly used sentence structure was the passive voice and was phrased in 'one would need to' or 'one should'. The lawyers put forth new concepts or ideas in subsequent sentences with infrequent building upon previous comments.

Thinking patterns

Business people provided space for 'experimental thought' as well as more elaborated ideas. They used personal stories or professional experiences to explore the commercial proposal, looking at how they would use or be attracted to the business offering. In so doing, there was personal ownership of ideas, a higher level of excitement, and they were less inclined to deal with the case in the abstract. Business people used their imagination to assess the business proposal using a variety of contexts as well as social and commercial trends, such as generational theory and changing paradigms of work.

Business generalists exhibited relatively no emphasis on qualification or perceived hierarchy in the group. This was supported through a conversational, free-flowing decision process. When summarising, they saw numerous possibilities for the new venture.

Lawyers moved into assessment of the business proposal only after defining the task so as to move forward from a common understanding. Throughout the session there was emphasis on the process, methodology and structuring of the session; frequent stops to ensure group understanding and consensus; and continual reassessment and questioning of the task to ensure it was being dealt with correctly.

Lawyers sought to base their decision on fact, available data and known market research. They took up the role of devil's advocate and assumed the most negative possible perspective to identify and then overcome any real or possible obstacles. In so doing, they dealt with the business proposal as an abstract task and evidenced no personal involvement in the business idea.

In the lawyers' group, a hierarchy based on apparent expertise was self-introduced, self-enforced and respected. This was accompanied by linear problem solving, and regimented and highly formatted discussion patterns. When summarising, they saw limited possibilities for the new venture.

Specific expertise contributed within a commercial context

Business people acknowledged and appreciated the complexity of the commercial scenario and explored possible ways of understanding the viability of the proposal. In contrast, lawyers firstly defined the proposal clearly and searched for the 'right' answer with direct and formulated views, deftly identifying and dealing with any risks.

Underlying values

The language and thinking patterns of business people and lawyers are indicative of the values of each group. Analysis of the stories told by members of each group about the benefits of their function revealed a great deal about their respective values. In the research findings, there was no overlap in values between the groups and each group accurately expressed several key values of the other. This suggests that in interactions between specialists and generalists, each group clearly exhibits and defends its own values. For example, both lawyers and business people assumed that lawyers were technical and managed risk (a 'safety net' or 'navigator'); while business people were practical, opportunity focused ('Can we do it?') and results oriented.

Responses to individual questionnaires supported each group's values profile. Business people responded that they were trained to put profit, the client and shareholders above all else. Their common fear about the business concept was related to loss of opportunity or failure to profit. Lawyers responded that they were trained to give priority to legal compliance, accuracy, practicality, reputation of the business and integrity. Their greatest fear about the business concept related to risk, damage to reputation and non-compliance of laws.

Commerciality: a way forward

The IKD commerciality research clearly suggests that the mental schema of lawyers and their business partners play a key role in creating a commerciality gap between them. In other words, specialists and generalists both practise valuable skills in identifying, assessing and implementing commercial opportunities. They each bring a unique skill set to the table — partly due to the fact that they are trained to carry out specific functions within an organisation. The unique behaviours of specialists and generalists suggest different underlying values which motivate and guide each groups' members in their interactions. This is a key cause of potential dissonance between the groups and it needs to be resolved to optimise commerciality.

Lawyers, as specialists, and business people, as generalists, need to recognise and leverage their differences to create a more commercially productive work environment. There is a risk in thinking the best way forward might be to mitigate the difference by encouraging each group to move toward the other and lessen the gap. The error in this thinking is similar to that of talking in averages; we lose the richness that comes with the full range of diversity. We compromise the outcome.

Perhaps a more productive and beneficial way of addressing the differences in behaviour is to establish a framework or process that recognises the divergent skills and values, and builds on the best of both. This bridge-building can be done by:

- identifying and valuing the skill set of other groups;

- clarifying the role each team member is playing in any interaction; or being transparent when you choose to put on a different hat or speak from a different set of values;

- avoiding exclusive terminology and jargon which alienates or confuses other groups;

- improving listening skills in order to recognise triggers for miscommunication;

- recognising and re-shaping structures built into the organisation that allow or encourage divergences; and

- identifying thinking patterns and dialogue habits that foster non-productive interactions and addressing them.

Summary

In-house counsel often hear the plea from their business partners, 'We need our lawyers to become more commercial'. This plea is for more than giving succinct advice, avoiding legalese, and understanding the business. It is a plea for participation in business discussions and decisions in a more engaged manner; one that takes into account the industry pressures, market trends, the financial impact of decisions and the competitive edge required for sustainability.

Lawyers' mental schema have not typically been shaped to work automatically at this level. By being aware of their schema and that of their business partners, in-house counsel can more effectively build communication bridges that optimise their strengths. By doing this consistently, they will earn a seat at the table.

---

1   David P Ausubel, 'Viewpoints from related disciplines: Human growth and development' (1959) 60 *Teachers College Record* 245–54.

2   Peg C Neuhauser, *Tribal Warfare*, Harper & Row Publishers, New York, 1988, p 5.

3   Edward T Hall, *Beyond Culture*, Doubleday/Anchor, New York, 1976.

4   *Building Commerciality Research Report 2007*, unpublished report, Institute of Knowledge Development, Melbourne, 2007.

10

PROFESSIONAL ETHICS: IN-HOUSE COUNSEL AS IN-HOUSE CONSCIENCE

by

Kirsten Mander

Kirsten Mander is General Counsel and Company Secretary of Sigma Pharmaceuticals, a leading Australian manufacturer of pharmaceutical products. In addition to her previous experience as general counsel for a number of other major private and publicly-listed companies, she was also General Manager for Strategy, Government and Regulatory affairs at TRUenergy, and is a director on several boards. Kirsten is a member of AICD and CSA. She is a former President of the Victorian division of ACLA, as well as a former council member and Chairman of the Ethics Committee of the Law Institute of Victoria.

Introduction

Among all the challenges faced by lawyers today, some of the most significant relate to the need to reconcile the demands of an increasingly fast paced, commercial world with the need to operate ethically and in accordance with legal professional duties. No lawyer is likely to finish their legal career without having had to grapple with some thorny ethical dilemmas along the way.

Events over the last few years have demonstrated the willingness of too many corporate managers to forget the fundamental principles of good governance. It is a basic tenet of corporate existence that a company's primary objective should be to enhance

141

shareholder wealth. However, in pursuing this, too often managers seem to lose sight of the fact that the company and all people within it are obliged to act within the boundaries set by the community and the law. Yet, even with a clear commitment to ethical conduct, finding where the real boundaries of acceptability lie is often a formidable task. This is partly because many of the factors are highly subjective, and partly because companies and their shareholders have a legitimate interest in testing those boundaries.

In-house counsel tend to have heightened exposure to these challenges due to their status as employees and, often, as members of the management team of the company which employs them. In addition, they also tend to have heightened levels of discretion in decision making, as well as access to informal sources of information which their private practice colleagues do not have.

Notwithstanding this, the professional and ethical duties of in-house counsel are the same as those of other legal practitioners. As Lord Denning MR noted in *Alfred Crompton Amusement Machines Limited v Customs and Excise Commissioners* [1972] 2 QB 102 at 129:

> They [in-house counsel] are regarded by the law as in every respect in the same position as those who practise on their own account. The only difference is that they act for one client only and not for several clients. They must uphold the same standards of honour and etiquette. They are subject to the same duties to their client and to the court. They must respect the same confidence. They and their clients have the same privileges.

It has been suggested that the peculiarities of the in-house counsel role mean that in-house counsel are less capable of exercising independence and maintaining professional standards than their private practice colleagues. However, this comparison seems to ignore the pressures on private practitioners who lie or die on six-minute chargeable units and monthly billings, and who often have very significant law firm revenue streams dependent on keeping their corporate clients happy. It also overlooks the fact that the role played by in-house counsel within their companies as promoters of ethics and good governance is generally highly valued by those organisations. In fact, in-house counsel can justifiably be proud that although they constitute between 20–30% of the entire Australian legal profession, almost none of the professional misconduct complaints each year are against in-house counsel.

Dealing with professional ethical dilemmas

Yet, despite the relatively clean record of Australian in-house counsel generally, recent corporate scandals such as HIH, Enron and the Australian Wheat Board (AWB) demonstrate the increasing degree of public scrutiny and criticism to which the conduct of in-house counsel is likely to be subject in the future. They also highlight the very severe potential consequences to the individuals concerned. This emphasises the imperative for in-house counsel to be fully aware of their ethical obligations, and to be ready to successfully negotiate these challenges if and when they arise.

What then at a practical level is the best way to approach an ethical dilemma? To illustrate this, we will take what many would say is the most difficult of all ethical dilemmas which face lawyers: what do you do if you know your client is guilty? Applying the same question to the in-house counsel context: what should an in-house counsel do if the counsel becomes aware that a company product may have deficiencies? What if they provide advice to rectify the situation, but the commercial manager they report to ignores their advice, or even directs them to cover up the evidence? In order to analyse and resolve these kinds of dilemmas, asking a number of fundamental questions can be very useful.

Who is my client?

The first question that should be raised when confronted by an ethical dilemma is this: who is my client? Generally, the client of an in-house counsel is the organisation which employs him or her. In the private sector, this means it is the company that an in-house counsel owes professional duties to.

However, this is only the beginning. The reality is that a company is a legal construct which is composed of a collection of different individuals with different responsibilities, including employees, directors and officers. None of these individuals is the client as such. Rather, they are all agents of the client — which is the company itself.

Who then represents the client for the purposes of determining the best interests or will of the company? In this regard, it is commonly the board of directors which is regarded as the governing mind for the organisation. The board, therefore, effectively represents the client.

Yet, even the board itself is composed of individuals who may have interests or views which are adverse to those of the company as a whole. Accordingly, some would argue that the true touchstone for measuring corporate interests must be the collective interests of the shareholders. However, the board of directors is the body which has been given the responsibility by shareholders to govern the organisation on their behalf. Therefore, in normal circumstances, decisions by the board (as the properly constituted decision-making body for that organisation) should be accepted by the in-house counsel.

What are my duties?

With respect to specific professional and ethical duties, in-house counsel are generally bound by the general principles of professional conduct which apply to all lawyers. In Australia, these principles can be found in large part in the relevant legislation and professional conduct and practice rules of each state and territory. In Victoria, for example, these would be the Legal Profession Act 2004 (Vic); and the Professional Conduct and Practice Rules 2005 (Vic). These duties can essentially be grouped under three categories: duties to the law; duties to the court; and duties to the client. Below, I discuss these three duties in greater detail and the additional duties an in-house counsel has under the Australian company legislation.

Duty to the law: First and foremost, lawyers have a duty to the law. Generally, in-house counsel must not:

- engage in conduct that is dishonest, illegal or unprofessional and which may bring the legal profession into disrepute, or which is prejudicial to the administration of justice; and
- knowingly assist or seek to induce a breach of law by clients, other practitioners or third parties. They may criticise the law, but must not do so in a manner which undermines the law or public confidence in it.

The duty to comply with the law applies only to the lawyer's conduct. It prohibits the lawyer from breaking the law, or assisting their client or others to do so. To return to our example, if an in-house counsel knows that the company's product is not living up to expectations and this breaches the law (for example, safety laws, trade practices legislation etc), the lawyer cannot assist the sale of that product.

This duty does not require the in-house counsel to prevent the company from breaking the law (although a lawyer's duty to the client would certainly require that the lawyer use his or her best endeavours to try and do so). Nor does it require the in-house counsel to disclose the client's illegal conduct to the responsible authorities.[1] In each case, the in-house counsel will have to consider how these matters can be reconciled with the lawyer's own personal ethical code, while keeping in mind the duties to maintain confidentiality and to act in the best interests of the organisation.

Duty to the court: In-house counsel, like all lawyers, are officers of the court. As such they have a duty to act with frankness, candour and honesty in relation to the court. The cardinal rule here is that a practitioner must not knowingly make a misleading statement to a court on any matter. Where in-house counsel is informed that the client has lied in a material particular, or procured another to do so, the in-house counsel must either, with the authority of the client, disclose this or else refuse to take any further part in the case.

To return to the previous example: even if instructed by their client, in-house counsel must not participate in the destruction of documents which are reasonably likely to be required in legal proceedings; in other words, they must comply strictly with the rules of discovery.

It should be borne in mind that this duty to the court is an overriding duty. Where there is a conflict between an in-house counsel's duty to his or her client and to the court, it is the duty to the court which must prevail.[2]

Duty to the client: In-house counsel must act in the best interests of their clients and exercise due skill and diligence, while maintaining client confidentiality and avoiding conflicts of interest.[3] If we return to the earlier example, what then is the duty of an in-house counsel when the supervising manager issues instructions which the counsel considers are unethical or in conflict with the best interests of the organisation?

The proper course of action for the in-house counsel will depend on the nature of the issue. Even where an in-house counsel is a member of a management team, that role on that team is not simply an extension of the role of the commercial managers in the company. The in-house counsel's role is to provide independent judgment and advice, and to act in the best interests of the client — that is, the company.

Our system of corporate governance has long relied upon the participation of independent parties (such as lawyers) who are bound to act in the best interests of their clients. This system of checks and balances is a fundamental element of the shareholder mandate and the community's licence to operate. As such, in-house counsel must use their best efforts to advise the company. This may entail raising the issue to senior management or the board. Indeed, an important, and sometimes the most difficult duty of in-house counsel, is to speak up and ensure that senior management and the board are properly advised. This is the case even if there is no request for advice or, worse, in the face of management opposition.

As noted earlier, it is the board of the company which is the ultimate representative of the client. However, this does not mean that all management decisions that an in-house counsel disagrees with should be elevated to the board. The best interests of the company are generally best served by management being permitted to manage within their authority levels (including making mistakes) without undue interference from above. This includes making difficult risk-reward judgments.

However, if there is a clear violation of the company's legal obligation and this is likely to result in a substantial injury to the organisation, then the in-house counsel has an obligation to take active steps to elevate the issue to the appropriate decision-making body and oppose that legal violation. As the American Bar Association Model Rules of Professional Conduct provide (R 1.13), this may require the in-house counsel to ask for a reconsideration of the matter, seek a separate legal opinion or refer the matter to the board. Ultimately, if all else fails, the in-house counsel may have no option but to resign.

It is worth reinforcing the point that it is the client who determines the scope of the retainer and consequently what the client's best interests are. It is not the role of any lawyer to impose his or her own values, ethics or risk tolerances on clients. It is the role of the lawyer to properly and fully advise regarding the consequences of a course of action, and to use his or her best endeavour to look after the client's interests.

On this point, there is a fine but important line between persuasion and paternalism. Provided that the appropriate level of management within the client business or organisation has a full understanding of the potential drawbacks of a course of action, and provided that the course of action is not in breach of a lawyer's duties to the law or the court, the lawyer's obligation is to proceed in accordance with the client's instructions.

Duties under the corporations legislation: In addition to the preceding three professional duties, Australian in-house counsel are also subject to duties under the Corporations Act 2001 (Cth). Senior in-house counsel will often fall within the scope of the definition of 'officers' in s 9 of this Act and accordingly share many of the same duties as directors. These include (as per ss 180–182):

- the duties of good faith, due care, diligence and skill;
- the duty to not improperly use their position; and
- the duty to not improperly use information.

All in-house counsel are also subject to prohibitions on (as per ss 1307–1309 and the Trade Practices Act 1974 (Cth) s 52):

- misleading a director or the board, including giving or permitting the giving of information to a director that is false or misleading or which has omitted a matter which renders it misleading;
- making false or misleading statements to ASIC;
- falsification, concealment or destruction of any books (for example, accounts, registers and records) of the company; and
- aiding the above by any act or omission, directly or indirectly.

This obligation to fully and frankly disclose information to the board and in particular the application of this duty to in-house counsel has recently been dramatically highlighted in two separate Australian matters involving in-house counsel.[4]

The first matter involved the James Hardie group of companies. Proceedings were commenced by ASIC in February 2007 against a number of directors and officers of the James Hardie group, including its general counsel and company secretary.[5] ASIC alleged that when James Hardie established its foundation to compensate asbestos plaintiffs, it had issued misleading statements such as that the foundation 'has sufficient funds to meet all legitimate compensation claims' and that it would 'provide certainty for claimants'. ASIC alleged that various officers of James Hardie — including the general counsel/company secretary — knew or should have known that the statements were misleading and that they failed in their due care and diligence obligations. In particular, ASIC alleged that the general counsel/company secretary breached his care and diligence duties under the Corporations Act 2001 (Cth) s 180(1) on a number of grounds including the following:

- he knew or ought to have known that material presented to the board and public were misleading;
- he failed to take steps to ensure that directors were advised of this and/or to seek further advice from the company's lawyers; and
- he failed to query a letter sent by the external lawyers.

The second matter revolved around the 2006 inquiry into certain Australian companies in relation to the United Nations Oil-for-Food program undertaken by Commissioner Cole ('Cole Inquiry').[6] In particular, when examining the AWB transaction with another company called 'Tigress', the Cole Inquiry raised the allegation that AWB's general counsel failed to properly advise his client. Commissioner Cole took the view that AWB's general counsel might have breached of the Corporations Act 2001 s 1309 by:

- furnishing, authorising or permitting information to be provided to a director of the AWB which was false and misleading; or
- failing to take reasonable steps to ensure that it was not false or misleading even if he did not know that the information was false or misleading.

In each case, I stress that it is early days. The James Hardie defendants may well not be found guilty and, in the AWB case, actual legal proceedings may not even be initiated against in-house counsel. I highlight them, however, because they are a very salutary warning which underscores the fact that in-house counsel may soon be joining their private practice colleagues in being sued. They are also a reminder that in-house counsel's obligations extend beyond merely avoiding misbehaviour and providing advice on request.

Signposts along the low road

So far I have outlined the key legal and ethical duties of in-house counsel. More details of these and other duties can be found in the

ACLA *Ethics for In-house Counsel Handbook*.[7] However, understanding these duties is not the end of the story. The next challenge for in-house counsel is translating that understanding into effective action within a corporate environment. In this section, I focus on some of the impediments to responsible action commonly experienced in organisations. As a starting point, it is valuable to recognise these impediments in order to avoid falling into veritable traps.

Groupthink

Groupthink describes the phenomenon which occurs when group pressures cause poor decision making by otherwise intelligent individuals. Social psychologist Irving Janis found that groups are especially vulnerable to groupthink when their members are similar in background; the group is insulated from outside opinions; and there are no clear rules for decision making.[8] This perfectly describes the decision-making environment in many corporations.

Janis has documented eight symptoms of groupthink which are useful to recognise. Where these symptoms are present, poor decisions are probably not far behind:

- the illusion of invulnerability;
- collective rationalisation;
- a belief in inherent morality: members of the group believe in the rightness of their cause and therefore ignore the ethical or moral consequences of their decisions;
- a stereotyped view of out-groups: negative views of 'the enemy' render effective responses to conflict seemingly unnecessary;
- direct pressure on dissenters;
- self-censorship;
- the illusion of unanimity; and
- self-appointed 'mindguards' who protect the group and leader from problematic information.

The 1986 *Challenger* space shuttle disaster is regarded as a classic example of groupthink. In that case, concerns about the O-rings in the space shuttle booster rockets were ignored; the disaster eventually occurred. On this score, it is interesting to read Griffins[9] description of how the decisions in the lead up to the disaster fit into Janis' model of groupthink.

Conversely, by recognising these symptoms of groupthink early on and working towards breaking through them, in-house counsel can play an enormously valuable role on the management team of a company. On this point, leading by example is extremely powerful. The reality is that most staff most of the time have a fairly good idea of what is right or sensible and what is wrong or reckless. But it is enormously hard for many to stand up and say 'white' when everyone else is saying 'black'. In this situation, we should not underestimate the impact a single person can have by demonstrating a willingness to ask questions or stand up for what is right. If people with courage make high profile, moral decisions, they give others the courage to do likewise. If they do not, others will take this as a green light for them to do the same.

The boiling frog

Another impediment to ethical action is delay and inertia. This can be likened to the old story of the boiling frog. It is said that if you drop a frog in a pot of boiling water, the frog will jump out straightaway. But, if you place the frog in cool water and slowly heat the water, the frog will stay inside the water until the water reaches boiling point and the frog is boiled to death.

This is a metaphor to illustrate how people may not notice gradual change which is leading to disaster until it is too late. In these cases, small doubtful decisions accumulate and opportunities to correct the course are let pass. Human adaptiveness means that perceptions of what is normal or acceptable shift over time, and misbehaviour becomes just 'the way things are'.

As the legendary investor Warren Buffet once commented:[10]

> The five most dangerous words in business may be 'Every[one] else is doing it' … In fact, every time you hear the phrase 'Every[one] else is doing it' it should raise a huge red flag. Why would somebody offer such a rationale for an act if there were a good reason available? Clearly the advocate harbors at least a small doubt about the act if he utilizes this verbal crutch.

The moral is this: it is important to first recognise signs of hot water and then turn down the heat. Do not procrastinate. Take action before it is too late.

A cunning plan

Is there anything ever so dangerous as a cunning plan? Intellectually challenging problem-solving tends to focus decision making around objective, scientific, left brain factors. Complex and opaque structuring often serves to insulate and distract decision makers from the implications of their actions in the real world. This can result in decision making that is technically perfect and morally flawed.

I am reminded of Owen J in his report on the HIH corporate collapse, where he was fiercely critical of the way that middle managers and their advisers, including the lawyers, behaved as mere 'functionaries', rather than taking responsibility for the matters they were working on. He commented: 'From time to time as I listened to the evidence about specific transactions or decisions, I found myself asking rhetorically: did anyone stand back and ask themselves the simple question — is this right?'.[11] Too often I think the answer is no.

On the wrong track going fast

A similar danger is when in-house counsel make decisions in a hurry without adequate time for reflection. This is another significant contributor to poor decisions. If your gut is telling you something is not right, that is probably a pretty good indication that you need to pause, take a break and, if necessary, talk it over with someone.

Friends in low places

As a general rule, in-house counsel must avoid conflicts of interests. When faced with an unavoidable conflict, in-house counsel must declare it openly and clarify the capacity in which they are acting. In particular, I wish to highlight the all-too-often request to give professional advice and assistance to staff. In considering such a request in-house counsel need to be very sensitive to the potential for conflict of interests.

In-house counsel must consider carefully before accepting confidential communications from employees because this may put them in conflict with their obligation to advise the company. If they do accept such communications, they must advise the individual concerned that they are retained by the company and have a duty to act in its best interests, and that this may mean disclosure of those communications to the company.

In-house counsel must also take care when both the company and an employee are sued. Frequently, there is considerable advantage to both parties if the in-house counsel assists both. In such situations, however, in-house counsel must at the outset (and continually as the matter progresses) determine whether their interests may conflict. If there is an actual or likely conflict of interests, in-house counsel must decline to advise the employee.

The abominable 'no' man

Most in-house counsel aspire to be 'solutions oriented'. However, this is often easier said than done. Delivering bad news is rarely easy and most of the world does not seem to appreciate the purity of logic for its own sake quite as much as lawyers do. Rightly or wrongly, once an in-house counsel is perceived as being excessively risk adverse or negative, it will be enormously difficult to get his or her advice heard. We have all met them at Friday night drinks — in-house counsel with permanent tire tracks across their forehead. The answer to this, of course, is not to become an appeaser, telling management what they want to hear. An appeaser, as the American writer Heywood Broun is once claimed to have said, is someone who 'believes that if you keep on throwing steaks to a tiger, the tiger will become a vegetarian'. This is stupid on so many levels.

Instead, anyone wishing to be a successful in-house counsel has to acknowledge that persuading and influencing skills are a key skill set. They must be prepared to invest time in developing and using these skills. When an issue arises, in-house counsel have to be prepared to devote as much care, time and skill to crafting the delivery of the message in the most influential manner, as to crafting the message itself.

Clever in-house counsel will use techniques such as identifying the underlying needs and finding the best available ways to achieve an acceptable outcome. A critical first step will be to demonstrate engagement with the needs and imperatives of the other party, including the industry or company pressures under which they are working, the competitive implications and the financial impact of the decision. Clever in-house counsel will use presentation techniques that fit the recipient's decision-making styles. In the book *Spin Selling*,[12] Neil Rackham describes how many people, particularly clever, experienced people, tend to see the link between problems and solutions all too clearly and often jump too quickly to solutions before the other party is ready. Instead, he recommends first using implication questions to help others see the problem as serious enough to justify the answer.

Investing in the future

As this chapter has shown, a big part of successfully navigating ethical challenges is being proactive and putting in the groundwork well in advance. It is in this regard that in-house counsel are in a significantly advantageous position over their private practice colleagues. There are a number of ways which are available for in-house counsel to invest in establishing and strengthening the groundwork within a company — ways which are typically not available to external lawyers.

Educating the team

The first and best way to prepare for a successful resolution of ethical challenges is through education. In-house counsel should be educating themselves, their staff, their teams and the personnel they work with to think about the implications of their actions and their legal and ethical obligations. When working with colleagues on a daily basis, they should take the time to explain the implications of a decision and some of the associated issues so that next time these colleagues are already aware of the issues.

Accumulating the trust bank

In-house counsel should also be making deposits into the trust bank. Develop a reputation for giving good, straight advice. Deal with mistakes with sensitivity and raise problems only when they genuinely are serious problems.

On this point it is useful to get specific agreement about the in-house counsel role up front. In my previous position, I asked my boss to articulate my key goals; he advised me that my primary goal was to keep him out of jail. When the moment came for a robust discussion around potential courses of action, it was helpful to remind him that this was what I was endeavouring to achieve.

Building better governance systems

Good governance systems are an extremely important underpinning of an ethical culture. Governance systems will ensure that information flows to the right people at the right time as a matter of standard practice. This means there is less opportunity for problems to breed in dark corners. Opportunities to elevate issues are built into the company's normal governance so that problems can be quickly escalated without individuals having to risk career suicide.

These systems will include regular reporting protocols to the risk committee and board regarding matters such as compliance; legal and regulatory risk; standard sign-offs from legal and other divisions on all major transactions; policies and procedures for key risk areas; code of conduct and whistleblower incidents; and mentoring programs. The governance structure should ensure that, wherever possible, the chief legal officer should report to a senior executive such as the CEO, and has recognised access and reporting lines to the chairman of the board.

In-house counsel can also play an enormously valuable leadership role in working actively to encourage values, culture and structures that encourage and reinforce the positive ethical aspects of behaviour and business practice. They should be working collaboratively to promote honesty and transparency. They should discourage cynicism. Instead, they should be incorporating ethical considerations into general organisational policies, management processes, performance systems and training and development programmes.

Looking for like-minded colleagues

It is also important for in-house counsel to grow their own networks in the organisation and to build relationships with others who have the responsibility for or interest in responsible ethical decision-making. They should ensure that there are open communication lines to elevate issues up to the chairman of the board if necessary. They should also bring in like-minded individuals at an early stage when an issue arises.

In-house counsel will usually have the relationships, positional influence and access to a fairly high level of executive decision making. This gives them a significant opportunity to play a leadership role in influencing the ethical standards adopted by their organisations. I strongly believe that in-house counsel should take up this challenge and work proactively to develop corporate cultures that genuinely embrace the values of responsible, legal and ethical business conduct. I believe it is not only an important element of the value proposition for the client company, but that it makes good personal and business sense and is a fundamental duty of our role as lawyers.

Summary

In closing, let me summarise the key messages that I have been attempting to convey in respect of how to ensure that you are best equipped to successfully operate as an ethical in-house counsel.

First, in all things prepare well in advance. In particular:

- Be aware of your duties, responsibilities and obligations under law. Read your state professional conduct and practice rules and the ACLA *Ethics For In-house Counsel Handbook* periodically in order to refresh your memory.

- Learn to recognise some of the signs of dysfunction in organisational behaviours and decision making.

- Educate the managers you work with regarding their duties and personal liability, particularly in relation to misleading and deceptive conduct.

- Build strong relationships of trust across the business and good lines of communication to one or more senior managers and directors to whom issues can be elevated if you need to one day do so.

- Encourage the development of policies and systems that underpin good corporate governance, ethical behaviour and information flows.

- Encourage the development of a culture of transparency.

- Develop your own skills in persuasion and influence.

- If the corporate culture is simply not supportive of ethical conduct, leave the organisation before it sucks you down.

Second, when an ethical problem arises, consider these steps:

- Analyse the problem:
  - Who is my client?

- What do my legal and professional duties require?
- What does my conscience require?
- Consider the key stakeholders:
  - What are their objectives?
  - Is there a different way of handling the issue?
- Seek the confidential advice of your colleagues and ACLA.
- Ensure that all due and proper disclosure has been made.
- Advise the relevant manager clearly of the risks associated with their actions, including real past examples which can help make the consequences tangible. Consider and acknowledge their own needs and imperatives.
- Plan how to deliver the message persuasively and, if desirable, engage respected senior external counsel to deliver unpalatable advice.
- Elevate the issue to a more senior manager and, if necessary, to the chairperson of the board.

---

1   Note, however, that in some very limited cases statute law may impose such obligations; for example, the Sarbanes Oxley Act in the United States.

2   See *Giannarelli v Raith* (1988) 165 CLR 543 at 555 per Mason CJ.

3   For more details on these duties, see Dal Pont, *Lawyers Professional Responsibility*, LBC Information Services, Sydney, 2001; R Cocks, *Ethics Handbook: Questions and Answers*, Law Institute of Victoria, Victoria, 2004.

4   See Zwier and Kirwan, 'Criminal risk in corporate practice' (14 March 2007) ACLA VCCD.

5   ASIC, 'ASIC Commences Proceedings Against James Hardie', Media Release 07-35, 17 February 2007.

6   The Cole Inquiry was completed in November 2006. For more details, see <http://www.ag.gov.au> then 'All topics A–Z', 'Oil for food'.

7   ACLA, Melbourne, June 2005. Available from ACLA or through the website <http://www.acla.com.au>.

8   See I Janis, *Victims of Groupthink*, Houghton Mifflin, Boston, 1972; and I Janis, *Groupthink: Psychological Studies of Policy Decisions and Fiascos*, 2nd ed, Houghton Mifflin, Boston, 1982.

9   See E Griffin, *A First Look at Communication Theory*, 3rd ed, McGraw-Hill, New York, 1997.

10 Memo, Warren Buffet to Berkshire Hathaway managers, 27 September 2006: see <http://www.mrwavetheory.blogspot.com> then search for 'memo to all stars'.

11 Owen J, *The Failure of HIH Insurance*, The HIH Royal Commission, Canberra, April 2003.

12 N Rackham, *Spin Selling*, McGraw-Hill, New York, 1996.

11

WHAT IN-HOUSE COUNSEL WANT FROM LAW FIRMS

by

Ronald F Pol

Ronald Pol is the Director of professional services consultancy Team Factors Ltd, based in Wellington, New Zealand. He was formerly President of CLANZ, a member of the governing council of the New Zealand Law Society, and group litigation counsel, then corporate counsel, for New Zealand's largest publicly listed company. Ronald has also acted as general counsel for public and private sector organisations.

Introduction

What do in-house counsel want from their law firms? Some say that because every client is different law firms should simply address each client's needs independently. This is partly true. Every client or in-house counsel is different, and the best firms will meet their specific needs individually. To infer, however, that there is no need to look at the issue of client needs more broadly is to miss a great opportunity. A better understanding of the client perspective at the broader level can add enormous value in meeting the specific needs of individual clients and new clients.

In this chapter, I will focus on discussing what is meant by 'client focus' and 'client perspective'. The main point is that understanding the client perspective is key to delivering value; and, further, that this differs — and in some respects is a step up — from the strong client-focus already evidenced by the best firms.

What in-house counsel want: value

In my experience, and based on years of research involving the general counsel of some of the largest companies and government departments in Australia and New Zealand, what in-house counsel want from their external lawyers boils down to three main things. Clients want their external lawyers to:

- *identify* what adds value to the client;
- *deliver* that value; and
- *demonstrate* that they have done so.

This is not surprising. After all, whether or not they consciously set out to do so, every client representative — including the general counsel — has to do these same things in their own role within the organisation. Whether expressed in formal key performance indicators or implicitly, they also need to identify what value they can best add to the organisation's objectives, then deliver that value, and demonstrate that fact. So it makes perfect sense for in-house counsel to ask this from their external lawyers as well. Interestingly, the fact that there is a shared interest means that there is a strong basis for real teamwork between the external lawyer and a client's in-house counsel.

If in-house counsel think that law firms are *not* doing these three things, they may come up with ways to try and make the firms do so. This is where the situation can get messy. From the perspective of law firms, it can sometimes seem that in-house counsel dream up odd requests. Some may be similar to those asked by other clients and some totally different, yet the essence is the same — an attempt to ensure that their external lawyers meet the needs of their organisation.

For example, when I managed the major litigation and dispute resolution function of New Zealand's largest publicly-listed company, one of the requirements I introduced for New Zealand and Australian law firms related to invoices. I felt that the traditional law firm invoice showed the amount of time spent but did not reflect the value delivered by application of that time. So, I asked the law firms I retained to render their invoices in a way that specifically identified, for each main task within a transaction, how their work helped advance 10 key value-drivers for my organisation.

From my perspective, the invoice format we developed was an important step to ensure that the legal work done by law firms was more consistently focused on what really mattered to the company. Even though I tried to involve them in developing the criteria and processes (albeit with varying degrees of success) the law firms might not have seen it this way, perhaps muttering about me being a difficult client creating yet another requirement to complicate their busy lives. But if they did so, they missed an important point.

The point in creating the invoice format was not to create unnecessary burdens. It was simply my way of asking them to articulate how they identified, delivered and demonstrated the value-add which their work contributed to my organisation, in terms that I could understand as the client, and in terms that demonstrated to my superiors the value delivered by the lawyers in ways that resonated more strongly with them than simply 'time multiplied by hours worked'. Did I think my system was perfect? No. I would have been delighted if one of the firms had developed a better means of demonstrating value, but none ever did rise to this challenge.

From client focus to client perspective

Digging deeper into the invoice format example above, it is clear that what I, as an in-house counsel, wanted from my external lawyers was a greater appreciation of my perspective as to what was valuable to my organisation. In essence, all I had invited them to do was to identify, deliver and demonstrate value.

This need to see things from the client's perspective cannot be emphasised enough. Many external lawyers think that having client perspective is identical to having 'client focus'. They often seem to interpret this as diligently meeting every demand and whim of each client. So, they:

- complete invoices in a particular way to satisfy the wishes of client A;
- record time in a special way for client B, with narrations for each entry that match client B's reporting systems;
- provide the one-page advice letters sought by client C;
- include ghost-written internal memoranda for client D's general counsel to forward to the CEO and board;

- attend the monthly group meetings for client E's in-house legal team; and
- regularly visit the factories, mines or plants of client F.

So it goes — for every demand, for every request, for every client. The inference in all this is that meeting client requests equates to being client focused, and this means having client perspective. But this may not be the case. In my experience, specific client demands often emerge from an underlying need (perhaps not clearly, if at all, even articulated by the client) for the external lawyer to identify, deliver or demonstrate value from the client's perspective.

For example, a client's request to visit its mines or plants is not merely a request to make that visit. It is an invitation for the external lawyer to understand the client's physical and operating environment so that the lawyer can provide legal advice and solutions that take into account that specific environment. Legal advice and solutions tailored to the client's specific circumstances and perspective clearly provide greater value. In other words, client focus is making the visit when requested, while client perspective is using the deeper understanding gained from such visits to deliver legal advice that more effectively meets the client's business needs.

Certainly, the lawyer who goes to the mine when asked (client focus) will inevitably be better placed to understand, and meet, the client's needs (client perspective), and will often do so in practice. In this way, lawyers are often very good at the second of the three factors mentioned above; that is, *delivering* value.

But when they send a bill that says 'it cost $X because it took Y hours' all they are *demonstrating* is how long it took, not how their work connects with the client's business objectives. And when lawyers' lives are ruled by timesheets and budgets, it seldom occurs to them to 'waste' non-billable time visiting the client's mines in the first place. If so, a unique opportunity to better *identify* what adds value, right from the outset of the transaction, is often also lost.

What clients want from their external lawyers is not client focus as such, but a deeper understanding of how clients view their world — the drivers, constraints and challenges they face. They want their lawyers to appreciate (but not necessarily agree with) their perspective. Once an external lawyer has understood the client's perspective, the advice and solutions provided will almost always be more customised and commercially oriented than before. Having client perspective thus helps to identify, deliver and demonstrate value.

Law firm branding: how do clients see law firms?

Before law firms can effectively translate a deep understanding of client perspective into stronger client relationships, they must also appreciate how clients perceive law firms, particularly their own firm and its main competitors. Understanding a client's perception of a law firm is part of understanding client perspective. On this score, the firm's brand is critical.

Yet, when external lawyers speak about branding, often they are thinking of their new logo or the re-design of their website. Or they give a passionate rendition of what they describe as a strong point of difference about their firm, using words like 'professional', 'innovative' and 'collegial'. Actually, these are not so much the firm's brand as elements of the brand's manifestation.

To get a real description of a law firm's brand we should ask what clients think of the firm. Granted, a law firm's own perception of itself can help shape clients' perceptions over time. Yet, in many respects, what clients perceive about the firm today *is* actually the firm's brand right now.

For example, if clients think a particular law firm is the best employment firm in its field, they will go to that firm when they need the best employment lawyers. Even if the firm's partners genuinely believe that the firm is the best capital markets firm, and if by any objective measure the firm truly is the best such firm, if clients consider the firm to be mostly an employment practice, then that is the firm's real brand. This is because clients choose to buy or not to buy legal services based on their own perceptions. True, law firms can influence those perceptions over time. However, the best starting point is usually to find out what clients really think of the firm and its competitors.

Over the years, I have been involved in extensive research on key brand attributes of law firms. The results of the latest research, involving approximately a quarter of the New Zealand legal profession across law firms and in-house roles, is outlined in Figure 11.1.[1] This graph depicts the average score from across all in-house counsel respondents and illustrates broad brand perceptions of the 14 largest New Zealand law firms according to organisational clients.

Figure 11.1

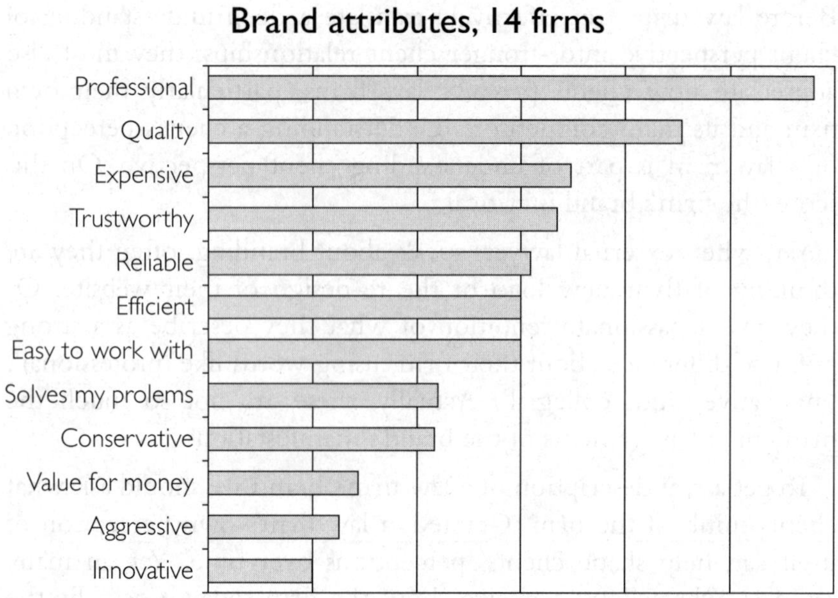

Brand attributes, 14 firms

Obviously, each firm differs in the manner in which it is perceived by key organisational clients. Yet, even at this highest level of abstraction with averages across the largest firms, the broad perceptions are telling. Professionalism is virtually a given. Quality, trustworthiness, reliability and expensiveness also rank highly. By contrast, however, value for money and problem solving rank relatively poorly. Also, large firms generally are not perceived as being particularly innovative, notwithstanding the marketing efforts and genuine belief of partners and business development directors regarding their 'innovative' practices.

This type of analysis differs from market brand perceptions research conducted with a firm's own clients. After all, from a law firm's perspective, if you really want to understand how better to serve another firm's clients, it is useful to have a good idea not just of the brand perceptions of your firm and how your clients might view your competitors, but also to know how those firms' clients view them. Nor is this type of research skewed by clients that have already selected your firm for their panel; it looks across all organisational clients with sophisticated operations and in-house legal functions.

It is particularly instructive to examine not only how a specific firm rates with organisational clients, but also how firms compare with their competitors. Figure 11.2 illustrates results for 10 large New Zealand firms specifically in relation to client perceptions of quality. Clearly, in clients' eyes, several firms are well ahead of their peers. Others are lagging, in some cases quite significantly. Viewing similar data across the full range of key brand attributes is also revealing, as it identifies areas of strength, as perceived by clients themselves, and areas for improvement — all this within the context of the clients' views of the firm and its competitors.

It is, of course, instructive also to know how individual firms are perceived by specific sections of the client base or wider legal community. For each firm, these data can, for example, be filtered by a wide range of factors such as gender, location, public or private sector, general counsel, senior counsel, or other factors.

Figure 11.2

Brand attributes: quality

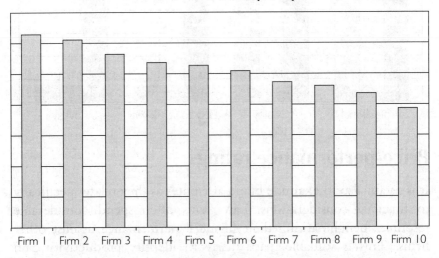

It might, for example, be expected that the firm's own lawyers have a particular perception about the firm, and this might differ from the perception of clients and their competitors. The evidence, illustrated in Figure 11.3, reinforces this expectation. In respect of one selected law firm, Figure 11.3 outlines the different perceptions of in-house counsel familiar with that firm (that is, its clients), other private practice lawyers (that is, its competitors) and the firm's own lawyers, across each of the brand attributes referred to.

The trend from Figure 11.3 is clear. On the attributes in this example, the firm's own lawyers rate themselves more highly than clients, and clients rate them more highly than their competitors. Interestingly for this firm, the difference is most pronounced in relation to innovation. It seems that the firm's own lawyers consider the firm to be particularly innovative — a view clearly not shared by the firm's clients or its competitors.

Figure 11.3

Comparative brand attributes, specific firm

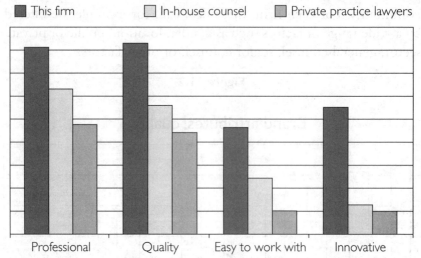

It is useful also to examine brand attributes as they relate specifically to financial considerations. Law firms often spend considerable resources benchmarking their financial performance against other firms. This is valuable, particularly to identify productivity gain opportunities. Yet, in the longer term, how a firm compares against its competitors, in size, leverage, utilisation rates, partner profits, etc, pales into relative insignificance against how its clients perceive the

Price-performance ratings

firm. After all, even the most efficient law firm might falter if its clients consider its performance lacking or its pricing wrong.

In the latest research (where around 30% of New Zealand's in-house profession participated) in-house counsel — as the primary client representatives for many of the largest corporate and government organisations — rated the law firms they use on overall performance and price. The findings are illustrated in Figure 11.4.

What is important here is not so much which quadrant a firm happens to be in, but whether this accords with the firm's own positioning strategies. The two firms furthest out in the top right quadrant, for example, may be perfectly happy to be considered expensive, because they are also regarded as delivering exceptional performance. In contrast, a firm that considers itself a top performer may find that clients regard it as expensive but not quite in the same 'performance' league as its competitors. This analysis provides an important reality check and the opportunity to address the issue before it is too late.

Figure 11.4

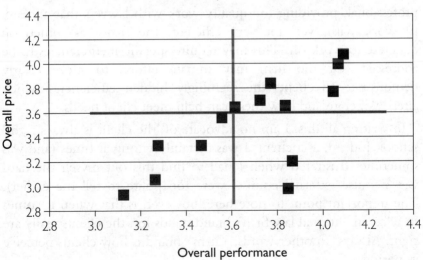

Price–Performance matrix
14 firms, rated by in-house counsel

Remove the filters: client perception is paramount

Any difference between a firm's own perceptions and those of its clients does not automatically mean that clients 'don't understand us', or that clients have 'got it wrong'. To the contrary, if we accept that a firm's brand is entirely what its clients (and prospective clients) consider it to be, any misperceptions rest solely with the firm itself.

The first step, therefore, is to accept the need to assess the firm's brand without using the rose-tinted spectacles of self-perception. Firms must also look beyond current profitability comparisons because these often reflect the outcome of past client perceptions, often built up over many years. Instead, they must focus on current client perceptions because this is what affects future profitability.

For external lawyers, it is not all gloom and doom if client perceptions are less than rosy. Thankfully, firms have the power to do something about it. Comparing last year's financial results with competitors' results will not change anything. Benchmarking clients' brand perceptions, however, provides opportunities to help shape client perceptions and, ultimately, affect future profitability.

For example, if a firm learns that clients consider the firm to be professional, providing top quality work with lawyers that are easy to work with, yet not very efficient, the firm has something concrete to work on. This may require specific inefficiencies to be addressed. Or the firm may initiate efforts to more clearly demonstrate to clients the seemingly hidden efficiencies which already operate and how these can help meet client needs.

In writing all this, I am no advocate of 'the client is always right' school. Indeed, as a client, I was certainly wrong at times (and was sometimes frustrated when I had to find this out myself the hard way because external counsel were too polite to tell me earlier). The important point to note here, however, is that when it comes to what an external law firm's brand stands for, the clients really are right. Always. In other words, a firm's brand is how clients perceive it, period.

Bringing it together: building client perspective systems

Based on client perceptions of a law firm's brand and a clear understanding of client needs, a law firm is in a good position to develop systems that deliver legal services in ways that meet clients' value perceptions, and build a firm's brand in a direction consistent with a firm's development strategies. This goes to the heart of what I mentioned earlier — that, essentially, clients and their in-house counsel want only three things from their external lawyers: that they identify, deliver and demonstrate value to the client organisation.

In my experience, most good lawyers deliver value well, ultimately achieving a great outcome as zealous and committed advocates on their clients' behalf. Yet, the process is often painful and seemingly unfocused from the client perspective. They may get the right result but only after many months, or years, of uncertainty and spiralling costs. Sometimes the legal process itself appears to drive decision making more than the client's commercial objectives. Not surprisingly, many general counsel continue to say that relatively few external lawyers truly identify the client's core objectives or their top value-drivers right from the outset.

This is, of course, especially difficult if clients themselves are uncertain of those objectives, as when they say: 'Here's my problem, please fix it'. This suggests that there exists an opportunity for law firms to distinguish themselves from their competitors. They can do this by consistently ensuring the early identification and consequent sharp focus on the client's core commercial objectives before starting work, or at least at a much earlier stage. The best way to do this is to build client perspective systems that consistently highlight client objectives and then deliver on them.

Anecdotal evidence suggests that some of the better lawyers are indeed now more conscious of the need to define client objectives earlier in the process. Unfortunately, however, even when they achieve a great outcome, few lawyers then adequately demonstrate the value of their contribution in terms that relate directly to the client's objectives. Instead, many lawyers demonstrate mostly the output of the legal process and the time expended to achieve that result.

In other words, many external lawyers have not created client perspective systems that effectively demonstrate the value of their work to clients, in terms of an outcome that directly resonates with the client's own objectives. This, by the way, never has anything to do with the time spent by lawyers getting to the goal. Unfortunately, time is typically the key internal law firm measure that is then translated to the client's bill. The problem is that when time, whether explicitly or implicitly, is used to measure 'value' this tends to reinforce perceptions of expense and inefficiency rather than delivering business solutions.

As an example, let me recount the following story from the general counsel of a large company. Broadly, in his words as I recall them:

> We engaged a law firm and merchant bank, both blue chip firms, for a major transaction of critical importance. As it transpired, the law firm undertook more of the work, took more risk, and probably helped us achieve our objectives more than the bank. Yet, when the law firm presented its fee invoice (for some hundreds of thousands of dollars), my CEO demanded that I query it. We eventually settled for less. Yet, the merchant bankers' fee, something like ten times as much as the law firm's fees, went through without a hitch.
>
> The difference? The bankers' fee was tied directly to our own value proposition for the transaction. Their fee was largely linked to the share price (incidentally, as was the CEO's bonus), and the CEO was delighted by the huge surge in shareholder value that resulted from the transaction — of which the bank's fee was a tiny fraction.
>
> By contrast, although the lawyers also spoke of the success of the transaction, their fee was linked only to the amount of time spent by the lawyers, in effect inviting the client not to reflect on success but on how much time was spent getting there. The CEO promptly recalled meetings in which five lawyers arrived for negotiations, and which dragged on endlessly over what he saw as technical legal issues raised by the lawyers themselves. I tried to explain the value of some of these discussions, but because the firm had expressed its own value in terms relating mostly to time spent, it was hard to argue with the perception of over-lawyering. The irony was that when the merchant bank also sent five bankers to a meeting, it was seen as demonstrating commitment to us, the client!

Like many law firms, when the particular law firm in the story presented its bill, what it demonstrated most clearly were the tasks performed and the time spent on the transaction. This left the client little else to focus on. In contrast, the bankers' fee expressly demonstrated value by linking their services to what mattered to the client — in this case a clear increase in shareholder value. By doing this, the bankers invited the client to focus on the success of the transaction, not on time spent.

This story is validated by our latest research in 2008. Client representatives from Australian and New Zealand corporate and government agencies that together spend more than $1 billion dollars on legal services annually, rated their lead Australian and New Zealand law firms.[2] These firms were rated highly on areas relating to expertise, reputation and technical legal skills; around three-quarters of respondents rated their lead firms as very good or exceptional in these areas. However, less than a quarter considered their lead firms as consistently identifying value-add from the outset of transactions. (This is not just any firm, but their lead firm; that is, the one they have already selected as the best firm for their work.)

Aligning law firm systems with the client dimension

Some lawyers do a tremendous job in many of these areas already, but what I am suggesting is that in order to identify, deliver and demonstrate value *consistently and systematically* to clients, law firm systems must be aligned with client perspectives.

In reality, this is far from common. Despite the rhetoric from law firm marketing machines and the deafening claims of 'client focus', some of the most extensive research repeatedly shows that for the most part few in-house counsel are truly satisfied with their external law firms. Why? It seems that the problem does not generally lie with the lawyers themselves. Clients often recognise their lawyers as genuinely committed to their best interests. The reality is that most firms use operational systems that actively restrict the ability for their lawyers to identify and demonstrate their delivery of great client service.

So we get the situation where law firm websites wax lyrical about focusing on client needs but, in reality, these same law firms' practice management methodologies continue to focus almost exclusively on issues relevant to the firm's operational systems rather than client solutions. For example, practice management tends to

169

focus heavily on internal issues like better use of leverage (lots of junior lawyers); disbursement recovery (passing on as many costs as possible); billable hours targets (lots of very stressed lawyers); and strategic pricing (aided by teams of consultants).

The important point to note is that these issues revolve around factors internal to the firm. They are generally driven by cost structures and per-partner profits. Although they are also necessary, they miss a vital factor — the client component. In other words, law firms are expert at measuring the cost (to them) of services provided. Yet, clients tell us they remain seemingly incapable or unwilling to demonstrate the value (to the client) of those services. Specifically, law firms — unlike some of their banking colleagues with earnings that even top lawyers only dream of — are relatively unsophisticated at demonstrating the value they provide, in solid, measurable, ROI terms understood by client CEOs, CFOs and in-house counsel.

A quiet revolution: legal department growth

Law firm attempts to get more out of their existing processes also seem to be proving less successful with clients. Natural barriers to the number of hours that lawyers can bill do seem to exist, notwithstanding valiant efforts to break through the 24-hour limit. The 'bill-time-and-anything-else-we-can-count' approach still pursued assiduously by many law firms may also be increasingly counter-productive to good client relations.

In response, some of the largest client organisations have now, in effect, largely given up asking law firms to change. Instead, they are building their in-house legal teams to do significantly more of the work traditionally performed by law firms. The latest research published in the *ACLA/CLANZ Legal Department Benchmarking Report 2008* appears to illustrate a quiet revolution that some firms might be too busy to notice until it is too late. For a variety of reasons, legal departments report that some of the best work is being gradually taken in-house. Anecdotally too, as this chapter was being finalised, several more general counsel — whose organisations operate with a reasonably compact team and extensive use of outside counsel — indicated that they have now also decided to grow the size of their legal teams significantly and in-source most of their legal work, including some of the most sophisticated work traditionally performed by law firms. It will likely be another year or so before their law firms start to notice, by which time it will be too late to do much about it.

The irony is that many law firms are already making strong efforts to be client-focused. They speak with clients frequently and invite clients to partners' meetings. They engage consultants to assist with client reviews and use client surveys to gauge result-focused responsiveness and flexibility. To top it off, the firm's lawyers add interest, enthusiasm and great personal chemistry.

Many in-house counsel, even from the most frustrated corporate and government clients, would agree that the best law firms do all of this very well. Yet, as noted above, the research suggests that law firms' views of client focus often emanate from their own perspective, driven by the number of hours worked and other elements of law firms' systems. In short, many law firms are still trapped within a firm-perspective client focus, with cost-based hourly billing targets at their core.

From a client's perspective, however, value is typically more important than cost. Client focus from a genuine client perspective — one specifically geared towards meeting organisational goals — is paramount.

Instead of pushing the limits of a system already reaching its physical (and for some lawyers, psychological) limits, those firms brave enough to adopt a new approach to client focus might actually help deliver the greater value that clients seek. They will also help some of their lawyers reclaim a few scraps of life outside work and, perhaps serendipitously, even herald the next profitability transformation sought by firms themselves.

Meanwhile, looking at current law firm systems and processes, the only real link to any concept of value to the client is often the professional dedication of lawyers. Almost always, this is strong. Often, though, this dedication generates value in spite of — not because of — the firm's systems and processes. I predict that the best firms of the future will systematically and consistently develop and embrace processes designed to generate and reflect value more effectively to the client; and actively support their lawyers to identify, deliver and demonstrate that value.

Removing barriers to value: hourly billing

The final point I wish to make on the question of what in-house counsel want from their external lawyers relates to removing barriers to value. I wish to highlight this point by posing a single question: do clients really prefer hourly billing?

Some lawyers say that their clients demand hourly billing. Absolutely, some do. And this is what makes it complex: even those clients who do not like hourly billing may ask about the number of hours anyway, often as some form of validation exercise. This forces law firms to the conclusion that they really have no choice but to stick with this system. Yet, beyond anecdotal evidence morphing into accepted fact, at the broader level the evidence seems to suggest that sophisticated clients really do not like hourly billing; but they seem as trapped as law firms themselves.

In a major 2008 survey of Australian and New Zealand general counsel responsible for the legal function of corporate and government agencies that together spend more than \$1 billion on legal costs annually, only 3% considered hourly billing the best basis for pricing legal services; the vast majority expressed concerns.[3] However, although concern about hourly billing was widespread, there seemed to be less consensus on the level of intensity of such concerns. This appeared to be due to uncertainty about viable alternatives. In particular, 43% considered hourly billing to be merely 'generally appropriate' (that is, 'not ideal, but we have not found anything better'). The same amount again regarded hourly billing as 'not very appropriate' (that is, 'rewarding inefficiency and providing no incentive for success, but little alternative') or 'not all appropriate' (that is, 'totally outmoded and try to avoid whenever possible').

These findings represent an opportunity for change. It seems reasonably clear that successful alternatives developed between the most concerned clients and the most innovative law firms will be viewed with very real interest by other clients. If so, the message is clear. Before blinkered adherence to hourly billing results in more commoditisation of legal work, lawyers might take a leaf from the bankers' book. Pricing should follow — not be perceived as obstructing — the provision of great legal advice.

In reality, most lawyers are genuine in their desire to add value to their clients. Equally, clients want law firms to do so. So what is the barrier that prevents the delivery and demonstration of value through law firm billing systems?

My guess is that law firms (and for that matter, clients) still look at legal bills pretty much as a zero-sum game, or a static pie. If a law firm takes a bigger slice, it is at the expense of the client. Similarly, discounted fees are viewed as letting the client keep more of the pie. The result is that one side feels it has lost something, or both feel they have lost, and the relationship is constantly strained. Clients and lawyers pitted against each other is hardly conducive to a team rowing in the same direction.

If law firms instead develop and institutionalise alternative (or at least complementary) practice management and billing systems that genuinely encourage the development of key brand attributes and empower their lawyers to leverage these client-focused attributes throughout the firm, it might help consistently identify, deliver and demonstrate the value that clients seek. It might also herald the next transformation (and next step in per-partner earnings) sought by firms. This is truly a win–win possibility.

The problem is that traditional time costing or billable hours has the advantage of being simple. Concepts like 'value billing', 'satisfaction billing' and 'client focus framework' are difficult to apply.

Equally, it is appropriate to ask how 'value' is to be rewarded. In my view, 'value' seldom means simply one particular result, despite popular misconceptions to the contrary. Sophisticated clients typically accept uncertainty and risk and understand that different results can arise in spite of everyone's best efforts. For this reason, as a lawyer-manager for a large company, I developed a checklist with 10 factors demonstrating value, and a recent attempt uses seven factors; not a checklist with one simplistic measure of value. For any system to work in practice, it must be sufficiently simple to use. However, not so simple that it becomes unfair because it focuses on just one factor without acknowledging also that the provision of well-focused legal skill and effort often has considerable value even when the desired business outcome is not achieved.

It has also been suggested that few lawyers would be willing to undertake significant work for a small fee because that was the price at which the client 'valued' the job. Yet, that is the whole point; if it does not add value, do not do the work. This inherent reality check is what is often missing from the present billable hours costing system.

Moreover, identifying value to clients should not mean that client representatives are necessarily the sole arbiters of value. Neither does it mean that value can only be determined (perhaps capriciously) after the event. In essence, value billing simply uses a price or pricing formula based on value to the client and which is agreed to by the lawyer from the outset: before work is done. This is much like the bankers who meet with their client to identify value at the outset of a transaction, and focus their work specifically on tasks that will deliver that value. Then, at the end of the transaction, their systems clearly demonstrate the delivery of that value in terms that resonate directly with the client's own value drivers.

Conclusion

In this chapter, I have tried to demonstrate that what in-house counsel want from their external lawyers is essentially to identify, deliver and demonstrate the delivery of value. To do this, law firms must begin with a clear understanding of client needs based on being client focused. The best firms then transition from a strong client focus to a deeper understanding of the client perspective. All this, combined with the objective recognition of a law firm's brand — that is, how the law firm is actually perceived by clients — will help provide a solid base on which to develop systems that consistently deliver legal solutions in terms that resonate directly with clients' own perceptions of value.

---

1   Research conducted by Team Factors Ltd, partially published in *eCLANZ*, July 2008 (the newsletter of CLANZ). The respondents involved in this research represent the primary client representatives for many organisational clients across the corporate and government sectors; nearly 30% of the New Zealand in-house profession participated in the research, including over 115 general counsel.

2   *ACLA/CLANZ Legal Department Benchmarking Report 2008*, available for purchase from ACLA in Australia: <http://www.acla.com.au>; or from Team Factors in New Zealand and elsewhere: <http://www.teamfactors.com/legaldepbench.htm>.

3   Ibid.

INDEX

Adaptability, 7, 14, 69

Attitude towards in-house counsel, 13

Australian competitiveness, 13

Australian Corporate Lawyers
Association (ACLA), 8, 67
benchmarking studies, 118
Ethics for In-house Counsel
Handbook, 149
National Mentoring Program, 10

Australian lawyers practising abroad, 8, 88

Australia's Big Six law firms, 8
incentives to retain talent, 9
loss of talent to overseas firms, 8

Branding of law firms, 161–4
client perceptions, 161–4
comparison of firms, 163, 164

Business challenge, 13

Career progression
corporate in-house counsel, 89–90
government in-house counsel, 89–90
turnover of senior executives, 90

Challenges facing legal profession,
8–11
independence and integrity, 10
loss of talent to overseas firms, 8, 88
staff attraction and retention, 8–10,
87–9
standing as true 'profession', 10

Challenges of practising in-house,
11–13, 19
accountability, 12
adapting to changing environment,
7, 14
business challenge, 13
business expectation, 11
client legal privilege, 11, 16
globalisation, 5, 11
government departments, working
for, 12
in-house/external work balance, 14
independence and integrity, 10, 11,
12, 19
individual accountability, 11
multiple roles, 12
outsourcing of work, 11, 19
personal liability, avoiding, 15
professional indemnity insurance, 11
public service, 12
staff attraction and retention, 14, 19,
87–9
work processes, 14

China
cost-competitiveness of exports
to, 13
global legal team, 102, 108

Circadian rhythms, 42

Client
dealing with, 80–1
duty to, 145–7
employer as, 96
focus, 159, 169, 170

Client — *cont*
  government in-house counsel, 95–8
  identifying, 26, 95–8, 143–4
  law firm brands, perception of,
    161–4
  perspective *see* Client perspective
  ultimate client, 97–8
Client legal privilege
  abrogation of, 16
  European Court of Justice view, 16
  in-house counsel, application to, 16
  lawyer not acting in legal capacity,
    11, 32
Client perspective, 159–61
  aligning law firm systems with,
    169–70
  building systems based on, 167–9
  client focus distinguished, 159, 169
  law firm brands, perception of,
    161–4
  paramountcy, 166
Coaching, 58
Cole inquiry, 148
Commercial-mindedness, 28–9
Commerciality, 129–40
  'C-suite', 129, 130
  IKD research, 135–9
  mental schema, 131–3, 139, 140
  partnering with internal clients,
    129–40
  specialist/generalist clashes, 133–9
Commercially-oriented legal advice,
  10
Communication, 79
Company secretary and general
  counsel, 35
Compliance, 5, 7, 15
  legal and regulatory, 24
  performance evaluation, difficulty
    of, 116
  role of in-house counsel, 15, 24
Corporate collapses, 5, 143, 151
  ethical dilemmas, 143
  whistleblowers or star-witnesses, 15

Corporate governance, 5, 7, 15, 32,
  141–8
  building good governance systems,
    154
  codes of conduct, 15
  design and oversight, input into, 15
  duties of company officers, 141
  duties of in-house counsel, 15, 32,
    142, 144–8
  impediments to responsible action,
    149–53
  obligations under Corporations Act
    2001 (Cth), 15, 147
  penalties and personal risk, 15
  performance evaluation, difficulty
    of, 116
  promotion of good governance, 15
  US Sarbanes-Oxley Act, 15
Corporate sector regulation, 5
  role of in-house counsel, impacting,
    59
Costs management, 33
Crisis management, 7
Criticism of company, 30

Decision-making, 31–2
  clients, dealing with, 80–1
  frameworks, 71–83
  leadership characteristics, 71–6
  organisational dynamics, 81–2
  role of legal team, 76–8
  strategic planning, 82–3
Duties of in-house counsel
  best interests of client, 145, 146
  confidentiality, 145
  client, to, 145–7
  conflicts of interest, avoiding, 151
  corporate governance, 15, 32, 142,
    146
  corporations legislation, under,
    147–8
  court, to, 145
  disclosure of illegal conduct, 145
  dishonest conduct, not to engage in,
    144

due skill and diligence, 145, 147

full and frank disclosure to board, 147

good faith, 147

law, to, 144–5

legislation and practice rules, 144

misleading statements, not to make, 145, 147–8

officers of company, as, 147

opposing legal violations, 146

professional and ethical duties, 142, 144–8

Email management, 43–4, 101

Ethics, 141–56

achieving acceptable solutions, 152

ACLA Ethics for In-house Counsel Handbook, 149

client, identifying, 143–4

conflicts of interest, 151

developing reputation of trustworthiness, 153

duties of in-house counsel, 142, 144–8

educating team, 153

future focus, 153

good governance systems, 154

impediments to responsible action, 149–53

independence and integrity, 10, 11, 142

international uniformity, 12

like-minded colleagues, seeking, 154–5

performance evaluation, difficulty of, 116

proactive approach, 150, 153

professional ethical dilemmas, 143–8

true profession, mark of, 10

External lawyers

autonomy, 26

branding of firms, 161–4

client perspective, 159–74

clients' perception of firms, 161–4

government use of, 86–7

hourly billing, 172–4

in-house counsel as client to, 27

management of, 28, 36

practice management methods, 169–70, 173

price-performance ratings, 164–5

relationship with, 27–8

transition to in-house counsel, 23–33

value, delivering, 158–9, 172–4

what in-house counsel want from, 157–74

External learning programs, 59

Fidelity funds, 18

Global legal team

Audit Committee, 103, 111

consultation, 108

email, 101

leading, 100–13

legal conference, 105

telephone calls, 107

telephone conferences, 101, 109

typical day, 100–13

Globalisation, 5, 11

Australian competitiveness, 13

increasing stress on practitioners, 25

role of in-house counsel, impacting, 59

uniformity of standards, 12

Government in-house counsel, 12, 14, 85–99

admission, 90

APS Code of Conduct, 91

cadetships, 89

career progression, 89–90

challenges, 12

client, identifying, 95–8

Crown as ultimate client, 97

differences from private sector, 92–5

external lawyers, using, 86–7

graduate trainee programs, 89

increase in number of, 14

lawyer overload, 92–4

Model Litigant obligation, 12, 91, 92

Government in-house counsel — *cont*
  moral courage, 98
  practising certificates, 90–1
  public servants, as, 12, 91
  recruitment and retention, 87–8
  rules of conduct, 91–2
  shadow legal branches, 94
  similarities with private sector, 86–92
  Supreme Court officers, 90, 91
  ultimate client, 97–8
  unique government departments, 94–5
  value of service, 86

Graduate Diploma of In-house Legal Practice, 10

Groupthink, 149–50

High-value work
  doing, 40–4
  identifying, 37–40

History of in-house legal practice, 4–7

Hourly billing, 172–4
  billable hours as performance indicator, 114, 116
  clients' view of, 172

IKD LegalScores, 120–6
  development of, 120
  nine metrics, 121–2
  summary graph example, 124
  three dimensions, 120
  using, 123–5

Impediments to responsible action, 149–53
  conflicts of interest, 151
  cunning plans, 151
  delay and inertia, 150
  desire not to be negative, 152
  groupthink, 149–50
  hurried decisions, 151
  procrastination, 150

Incentives to retain talent, 9

Increase in number of in-house counsel, 3–4, 8, 14, 170–1

Independence and integrity, 10, 11, 12, 19, 142

In-house counsel work
  company secretary, 35
  complexity, 40
  doing valuable work, 40–4
  identifying valuable work, 37–40
  nature of, 35–7
  technical skills, 36

In-house/external work balance, 14

In-house legal team
  building team capability, 57–9
  communication with, 79
  ethics education, 153
  global, 100–13
  leadership *see* Leadership
  recruiting members, 78
  role of, 76–8
  team building skills, 36

In-sourcing legal work, 4

Integrated legal advice, 12

Internal learning programs, 58

Keeping up to date
  business thinking and writing, 67
  developments in law, 29

Key point-persons, 14
  Large Law Firm Group, 18

Law Council of Australia, 18
  capitation fees paid to, 18
  no in-house counsel representation, 18

Law firms *see* External lawyers

Law societies, 8, 18

Leadership, 65–84
  advocating company position, 77
  ambiguity, contradictions and risk, 75
  apologising, 75
  business publications, subscribing to, 67
  'change is an opportunity' culture, 68

characteristics of, 66–70
clients, dealing with, 80–1
communication with team, 79
decision-making frameworks, 71–83
developing style, 73
enjoyment of role, 71
ethical strength, 69
evolving, 72
feedback, 74
global legal team, 100–13
hard work, 76
keeping up to date with business
    thinking and writing, 67
knowing when to argue a point, 75
leading by example, 72
learning from mistakes, 68
legal excellence, 69
'let's try this' approach, 68–9
making others look good, 73
management style, 78–9
need for, 66
organisational dynamics, 81–2
outward looking attitude, 67–8
questions rather than accusations, 74
recruiting team members, 78
role of legal team, 76–8
shaping external environment, 67,
    69
shaping internal environment,
    69–70
strategic, 65–84
strategic planning, 82–3
understanding of business theory,
    67
varying style to suit audience, 72
wanting to lead, 71
working to make yourself
    redundant, 72
Legal proceedings
    prohibition from publicly
        commenting on, 17
Legal profession regulation
    Model Bill and Regulations, 17–18
    national approach, push for, 18
    State reviews, 18
Legal services market regulation, 10

Managerial functions, 32–3
Mental schema, 131–3, 139, 140
Mentoring, 58
Misleading statements
    duty not to make, 145, 147–8
Model Litigant obligation, 12, 91, 92
Model Rules of Professional
    Conduct, 17

National Legal Profession Model Bill
    and Regulations, 17–18
National Mentoring Program, 10

Partnering with internal clients, 36,
    129–40
    IKD commerciality research, 135–9
    language and dialect, 137
    mental schema, 131–3, 139, 140
    specialist/generalist clashes, 133–9
    thinking patterns, 137–8
    underlying values, 138
Partnership
    incentives to retain lawyers for, 9
    meritocracy, 9
People management skills, 27, 51–7
    learning, 54–7
    need for, 52–4
    perceived lack of, 51
Percentage of lawyers practising
    in-house, 3, 14
Performance evaluation, 114–26
    ACLA surveys and studies, 118, 119
    benchmarking tools, 118–20
    billable hours as traditional method,
        114, 116
    challenge for in-house legal teams,
        115
    CLANZ surveys and studies, 118,
        119
    cost efficiency, 116
    hurdles, 115–17
    IKD LegalScores, 120–6
    KPIs and KRAs, 118, 119, 122
    metrics, 118–20

Performance evaluation — *cont*
  non-revenue generating activities,
    116
  value/cost distinction, 6, 116
Personal liability
  avoiding, 15–16
  insurance against, 16
Practising certificates, 17, 90–1
  corporate in-house counsel, 90
  government in-house counsel, 90
  requirement to hold, 17, 90
  unrestricted, 17
Price-performance ratings, 164–5
Professional development, 47–60
  areas of current difficulty, 50
  areas of future difficulty, 50
  black-letter law CLE sessions, 48
  building team capability, 57–9
  coaching, 58
  emotional safety, 56
  external learning programs, 59
  formal, 49
  how lawyers learn, 57
  IKD research, 49–52
  informal, 49
  internal learning programs, 58
  learning soft skills, 54–7
  mentoring, 58
  people management skills, 51, 52–4
  raising effectiveness, 52–4
  'reflective practitioner', 54–5
  risk taking, 55–6
  self-assessment, 56
  soft skills, 52–7
  survey of needs of in-house lawyers,
    49–52
  transition from external to in-house
    counsel, 53–4
  trends impacting role of in-house
    counsel, 59
  what is, 48–9
Professional ethics *see* Ethics
Professional indemnity insurance
  lawyer not acting in legal capacity,
    11

Professional misconduct complaints,
  142
Public service
  government in-house counsel *see*
    Government in-house counsel
  values, 91

Reasons for working in-house, 25
Recruitment and retention
  cadetships, 89
  challenges facing legal profession,
    8–10
  corporate in-house counsel, 87–9
  global legal team, 109–10
  government in-house counsel, 87–9
  graduate trainee programs, 89
  in-house counsel, 14, 19
  incentives to retain talent, 9
  loss of talent to overseas firms, 8, 88
Remuneration
  incentives to retain talent, 9
  narrowing of gap between in-house
    and external practitioners, 25
Risk management, 7
  anticipating future risk, 12
  performance evaluation, difficulty
    of, 116
Risk taking, 31–2, 55
  acceptable solutions, 152
  conservative approach, 55
  risk averse nature of legal role, 55,
    152
Role of in-house counsel
  business objective, helping to
    achieve, 25
  commercial-mindedness, 28–9,
    129–40
  company employee, 30–1
  complex legal work, 24
  costs management, 33
  decision making, 31–2
  increase in, 24
  insider, 30–1
  involvement in business, 11, 25–6
  learning non-legal matters, 31

less autonomy, 26
management, 32–3
people skills, 27, 51
relationship with external counsel, 27–8
risk taking, 31–2
specialisation, 24, 134
traditional view, 23
trends impacting, 59–60
understanding needs of company, 31
Rules of conduct
corporate in-house counsel, 91–2
government in-house counsel, 91–2
Model Litigant obligation, 12, 91, 92
Model Rules of Professional Conduct, 17

Self-defence measures, 15–16
Senior Counsel
use of title, 17
Soft skills, 52–7
learning, 54–7
need for, 52–4
Staff attraction and retention, 8–9
State reviews of legal profession, 18
Strategic leadership see Leadership
Strategic planning, 82–3
Supreme Courts
government in-house lawyers admitted to, 90
rules of conduct, 91

Team building, 36
Time margins, 43
Transition from external to in-house counsel, 23–33
behavioural changes, 26
new skills required, 53–4
understanding expectations, 25

United Kingdom
global legal team, 102, 104

loss of talent to, 8
'Magic Circle' of law firms, 8
United States
global legal team, 110
Sarbanes–Oxley Act, 15
sub-prime crisis, 13
'White Shoe' law firms, 8

Value, 5, 6, 7, 8
billing systems, 173
client perspective, 159–74
cost/value distinction, 6, 116
external lawyers, from, 158–9, 172–4
government in-house counsel, 86
hourly billing, 172–4
invoices reflecting, 158–9
price-performance ratings, 164–5
removing barriers to, 172–4

Whistleblowers, 15
Work processes, 14
Workflow assessment, 37
Working hours, 14, 34–5
Workload management, 34–45
afternoon malaise, 42
briefing out routine work, 28, 37
circadian rhythms, 42
doing valuable work, 40–4
email management, 43–4
expectations and priorities, 39–40
high-value work, 37–40
identifying valuable work, 37–40
nature of in-house counsel work, 35–7
time margins, 43
urgent/important matrix, 41–2
workflow assessment, 37
workflow models, 38
Wrongdoing by company employees
ethical dilemmas see Ethics
impediments to responsible action, 149–53
lack of objectivity, 26–7
whistleblowers or star witnesses, 15